TEACHER'S PET PUBLICATIONS

PUZZLE PACK
for
Izzy, Willy-Nilly

based on the book by
Cynthia Voigt

Written by
Mary B. Collins

© 2006 Teacher's Pet Publications
All Rights Reserved

The materials in this packet are copyrighted
by Teacher's Pet Publications, Inc.

These pages may be duplicated by the purchaser
for use in the purchaser's own classroom.

Copying any of these materials and distributing them
for any other purpose is a violation of the copyright laws.

© 2006 Teacher's Pet Publications, Inc.
www.tpet.com

INTRODUCTION
If you already own the LitPlan for this title, this Puzzle Pack will refresh your Unit Resource Materials and Vocabulary Resource Materials sections plus give you additional materials you can substitute into the tests. If you do not already have a complete LitPlan, these pages will give you some supplemental materials to use with your own plan. There are two main groups of materials: one set for unit words (such as characters' names, symbols, places, etc.) and one set for vocabulary words associated with the book.

WORD LIST
There is a word list for both the unit words and the vocabulary words. These lists show you which words are being used in the materials and the clues or definitions being used for those words. You may want to give students a word list with clues/definitions to help them, or you may want students to only have a word list (without clues/definitions) if you want them to work a little harder. Both are available for duplication. The word lists can also be your "calling key" for the bingo games.

FILL IN THE BLANK AND MATCHING
There are 4 each of the fill in the blank and matching worksheets for both the unit and vocabulary words. These pages can be used either as extra worksheets for students or as objective parts of a unit test. They can be done individually if students need extra help or as a whole class activity to review the material covered.

MAGIC SQUARES
The magic squares not only reinforce the material covered but also work on reasoning and math skills. Many teachers have told us that their students really enjoy doing these!

WORD SEARCH PUZZLES
The word search words go in all directions, as indicated on your answer keys. Two of the word search puzzles have the clues listed rather than the words. This makes the puzzle a little more difficult, but it reinforces the material better. Two word search puzzles have words only for students who find the clue puzzles too difficult.

CROSSWORD PUZZLES
Both unit and vocabulary word sections have 4 crossword puzzles.

BINGO CARDS
There are 32 individual bingo cards for the unit words and 32 individual bingo cards for the vocabulary words. You can use your word list as a "call list," calling the words at random and marking them off of your list as you go, or you could use the flash cards by cutting them apart and drawing the words at random from a hat (or box or whatever). To make a better review, you might ask for the definition and spelling of each word as you call it out–or you could call out the definitions and have students tell you the words they need to look for on the puzzle.

JUGGLE LETTERS
The vocabulary juggle letter game is intended to help students learn the spellings of the words. One sheet has the definitions listed on it as an extra help for students who need it or to reinforce the definitions if you choose to do so.

FLASH CARDS
We've included a set of vocabulary flash cards you can duplicate, cut, and fold for your students. Some teachers make a few sets for general use by the class; others make a set for each student. Some teachers duplicate them for each student and have the students cut & fold their own. You can cut out just the words and put them in a hat, have each student pick out one word and write the definition and a sentence for that word. Students then swap words and papers, with the next student adding a sentence of his own under the last one. You can have students swap as many times as you like. Each time the student will read the sentences written prior to his own and then add a sentence. You can cut out the words and definitions separately and play "I Have; Who Has?" Each student in the room draws a word and definition. The first student says, "I have (the name of the word). Who has the definition?" The student with the definition reads it then says, "I have (the name of the vocabulary word she has). Who has the definition?" The round continues until all words and definitions have been given.

Izzy, Willy-Nilly Unit Word List

No.	Word	Clue/Definition
1.	ADELIA	Izzy's physical therapy nurse
2.	BATIK	Rosamunde hangs an animal ___ on the hospital wall.
3.	BEDROOM	Izzy moves into her parents' on the first floor.
4.	BRAINS	According to Joel, Jack underestimates Izzy's.
5.	CHEERLEADER	Former extra-curricular activity Izzy participated in
6.	CLINGER	Mrs. Lingard describes Rosamunde as a ___.
7.	CRUTCHES	Little Izzy did a back flip when Tony forgot to bring Izzy these.
8.	CRY	Lingards don't do this.
9.	DEBORAH	Tony's girlfriend
10.	DORA	Dr. Epstein compares Izzy to this Dickens character
11.	DRUNK	Word describing Marco when he drove Izzy home
12.	EPSTEIN	Doctor who is Izzy's pediatrician
13.	FRANCIE	Izzy's little sister
14.	GRIGGERS	Marco's last name
15.	HAIRCUT	What Izzy wants to give Rosamunde for Christmas
16.	HUMILIATED	How Izzy feels when she falls at school
17.	JACK	Twin brother who does not visit Izzy in the hospital
18.	JEALOUS	Francie had been ___ of Izzy before the accident.
19.	JOEL	Twin brother who does visit Izzy
20.	LATIN	Club Izzy misses
21.	LAUREN	Friend who avoids Izzy
22.	LEFT	The row of ___ shoes in the closet makes Rosamunde laugh.
23.	LEG	Half of Izzy's right one was amputated.
24.	LINGARD	Izzy's last name
25.	LITTLE	Izzy envisions ___ Izzy in her mind.
26.	LOOKS	Mrs. Lingard thinks Rosamunde must be uncomfortable because of the way she ___.
27.	MARCO	He was responsible for the car accident.
28.	MOTHER	A good ___ would stay.
29.	NICE	Word describing Izzy
30.	PENS	Izzy wants to borrow Francie's
31.	PIZZA	Food Izzy wants to eat when she gets home
32.	POOL	Mr. Lingard wants to put one in the back yard
33.	ROMEO	The assignment for ___ & Juliet gives Izzy trouble.
34.	ROSAMUNDE	Smart girl who becomes Izzy's friend
35.	SHOES	Mrs. Lingard removed all of Izzy's right ones from the closet.
36.	SUZY	She calls Izzy to see if Izzy is going to tell that Marco had been drinking.
37.	THERAPIST	Mrs. Hughes-Pincke, for example
38.	TONY	He invites Izzy to join the newspaper staff
39.	TREASURE	Place to buy handmade crafts: ___ Trove
40.	TREE	Object the car ran into
41.	TRIVIAL	Game Izzy, her siblings, & Rosamunde play: ___ Pursuit
42.	WEBBER	Rosamunde's last name

Izzy, Willy-Nilly Fill In The Blanks 1

_____ 1. Object the car ran into

_____ 2. Place to buy handmade crafts: ___ Trove

_____ 3. A good ___ would stay.

_____ 4. Game Izzy, her siblings, & Rosamunde play: ___ Pursuit

_____ 5. Francie had been ___ of Izzy before the accident.

_____ 6. According to Joel, Jack underestimates Izzy's.

_____ 7. What Izzy wants to give Rosamunde for Christmas

_____ 8. Mr. Lingard wants to put one in the back yard

_____ 9. Mrs. Lingard removed all of Izzy's right ones from the closet.

_____ 10. Tony's girlfriend

_____ 11. Club Izzy misses

_____ 12. The row of ___ shoes in the closet makes Rosamunde laugh.

_____ 13. Mrs. Lingard describes Rosamunde as a ___.

_____ 14. Smart girl who becomes Izzy's friend

_____ 15. Izzy envisions ___ Izzy in her mind.

_____ 16. Izzy moves into her parents' on the first floor.

_____ 17. Mrs. Lingard thinks Rosamunde must be uncomfortable because of the way she ___.

_____ 18. The assignment for ___ & Juliet gives Izzy trouble.

_____ 19. Word describing Marco when he drove Izzy home

_____ 20. Twin brother who does visit Izzy

Izzy, Willy-Nilly Fill In The Blanks 1 Answer Key

TREE	1. Object the car ran into
TREASURE	2. Place to buy handmade crafts: ___ Trove
MOTHER	3. A good ___ would stay.
TRIVIAL	4. Game Izzy, her siblings, & Rosamunde play: ___ Pursuit
JEALOUS	5. Francie had been ___ of Izzy before the accident.
BRAINS	6. According to Joel, Jack underestimates Izzy's.
HAIRCUT	7. What Izzy wants to give Rosamunde for Christmas
POOL	8. Mr. Lingard wants to put one in the back yard
SHOES	9. Mrs. Lingard removed all of Izzy's right ones from the closet.
DEBORAH	10. Tony's girlfriend
LATIN	11. Club Izzy misses
LEFT	12. The row of ___ shoes in the closet makes Rosamunde laugh.
CLINGER	13. Mrs. Lingard describes Rosamunde as a ___.
ROSAMUNDE	14. Smart girl who becomes Izzy's friend
LITTLE	15. Izzy envisions ___ Izzy in her mind.
BEDROOM	16. Izzy moves into her parents' on the first floor.
LOOKS	17. Mrs. Lingard thinks Rosamunde must be uncomfortable because of the way she ___.
ROMEO	18. The assignment for ___ & Juliet gives Izzy trouble.
DRUNK	19. Word describing Marco when he drove Izzy home
JOEL	20. Twin brother who does visit Izzy

Izzy, Willy-Nilly Fill In The Blanks 2

_____ 1. Smart girl who becomes Izzy's friend

_____ 2. Mrs. Hughes-Pincke, for example

_____ 3. A good ___ would stay.

_____ 4. Izzy wants to borrow Francie's

_____ 5. Food Izzy wants to eat when she gets home

_____ 6. Mrs. Lingard thinks Rosamunde must be uncomfortable because of the way she ___.

_____ 7. Dr. Epstein compares Izzy to this Dickens character

_____ 8. Word describing Marco when he drove Izzy home

_____ 9. Mrs. Lingard removed all of Izzy's right ones from the closet.

_____ 10. Marco's last name

_____ 11. Izzy's last name

_____ 12. Object the car ran into

_____ 13. Doctor who is Izzy's pediatrician

_____ 14. Little Izzy did a back flip when Tony forgot to bring Izzy these.

_____ 15. Friend who avoids Izzy

_____ 16. Half of Izzy's right one was amputated.

_____ 17. Rosamunde hangs an animal ___ on the hospital wall.

_____ 18. According to Joel, Jack underestimates Izzy's.

_____ 19. Rosamunde's last name

_____ 20. Club Izzy misses

Izzy, Willy-Nilly Fill In The Blanks 2 Answer Key

ROSAMUNDE	1. Smart girl who becomes Izzy's friend
THERAPIST	2. Mrs. Hughes-Pincke, for example
MOTHER	3. A good ___ would stay.
PENS	4. Izzy wants to borrow Francie's
PIZZA	5. Food Izzy wants to eat when she gets home
LOOKS	6. Mrs. Lingard thinks Rosamunde must be uncomfortable because of the way she ___.
DORA	7. Dr. Epstein compares Izzy to this Dickens character
DRUNK	8. Word describing Marco when he drove Izzy home
SHOES	9. Mrs. Lingard removed all of Izzy's right ones from the closet.
GRIGGERS	10. Marco's last name
LINGARD	11. Izzy's last name
TREE	12. Object the car ran into
EPSTEIN	13. Doctor who is Izzy's pediatrician
CRUTCHES	14. Little Izzy did a back flip when Tony forgot to bring Izzy these.
LAUREN	15. Friend who avoids Izzy
LEG	16. Half of Izzy's right one was amputated.
BATIK	17. Rosamunde hangs an animal ___ on the hospital wall.
BRAINS	18. According to Joel, Jack underestimates Izzy's.
WEBBER	19. Rosamunde's last name
LATIN	20. Club Izzy misses

Izzy, Willy-Nilly Fill In The Blanks 3

1. Francie had been ___ of Izzy before the accident.
2. Rosamunde hangs an animal ___ on the hospital wall.
3. Mrs. Lingard thinks Rosamunde must be uncomfortable because of the way she ___.
4. Little Izzy did a back flip when Tony forgot to bring Izzy these.
5. Word describing Marco when he drove Izzy home
6. Izzy envisions ___ Izzy in her mind.
7. Mrs. Lingard removed all of Izzy's right ones from the closet.
8. Club Izzy misses
9. Twin brother who does visit Izzy
10. Izzy's little sister
11. Mr. Lingard wants to put one in the back yard
12. What Izzy wants to give Rosamunde for Christmas
13. Dr. Epstein compares Izzy to this Dickens character
14. Former extra-curricular activity Izzy participated in
15. According to Joel, Jack underestimates Izzy's.
16. A good ___ would stay.
17. Izzy's last name
18. The assignment for ___ & Juliet gives Izzy trouble.
19. Smart girl who becomes Izzy's friend
20. Friend who avoids Izzy

Izzy, Willy-Nilly Fill In The Blanks 3 Answer Key

JEALOUS	1. Francie had been ___ of Izzy before the accident.
BATIK	2. Rosamunde hangs an animal ___ on the hospital wall.
LOOKS	3. Mrs. Lingard thinks Rosamunde must be uncomfortable because of the way she ___.
CRUTCHES	4. Little Izzy did a back flip when Tony forgot to bring Izzy these.
DRUNK	5. Word describing Marco when he drove Izzy home
LITTLE	6. Izzy envisions ___ Izzy in her mind.
SHOES	7. Mrs. Lingard removed all of Izzy's right ones from the closet.
LATIN	8. Club Izzy misses
JOEL	9. Twin brother who does visit Izzy
FRANCIE	10. Izzy's little sister
POOL	11. Mr. Lingard wants to put one in the back yard
HAIRCUT	12. What Izzy wants to give Rosamunde for Christmas
DORA	13. Dr. Epstein compares Izzy to this Dickens character
CHEERLEADER	14. Former extra-curricular activity Izzy participated in
BRAINS	15. According to Joel, Jack underestimates Izzy's.
MOTHER	16. A good ___ would stay.
LINGARD	17. Izzy's last name
ROMEO	18. The assignment for ___ & Juliet gives Izzy trouble.
ROSAMUNDE	19. Smart girl who becomes Izzy's friend
LAUREN	20. Friend who avoids Izzy

Izzy, Willy-Nilly Fill In The Blanks 4

_____ 1. Club Izzy misses

_____ 2. Mr. Lingard wants to put one in the back yard

_____ 3. Friend who avoids Izzy

_____ 4. Place to buy handmade crafts: ___ Trove

_____ 5. Twin brother who does visit Izzy

_____ 6. Former extra-curricular activity Izzy participated in

_____ 7. Mrs. Lingard describes Rosamunde as a ___.

_____ 8. The assignment for ___ & Juliet gives Izzy trouble.

_____ 9. A good ___ would stay.

_____ 10. Little Izzy did a back flip when Tony forgot to bring Izzy these.

_____ 11. Twin brother who does not visit Izzy in the hospital

_____ 12. According to Joel, Jack underestimates Izzy's.

_____ 13. Mrs. Lingard removed all of Izzy's right ones from the closet.

_____ 14. How Izzy feels when she falls at school

_____ 15. She calls Izzy to see if Izzy is going to tell that Marco had been drinking.

_____ 16. The row of ___ shoes in the closet makes Rosamunde laugh.

_____ 17. He invites Izzy to join the newspaper staff

_____ 18. Dr. Epstein compares Izzy to this Dickens character

_____ 19. Izzy's little sister

_____ 20. Marco's last name

Izzy, Willy-Nilly Fill In The Blanks 4 Answer Key

LATIN	1. Club Izzy misses
POOL	2. Mr. Lingard wants to put one in the back yard
LAUREN	3. Friend who avoids Izzy
TREASURE	4. Place to buy handmade crafts: ___ Trove
JOEL	5. Twin brother who does visit Izzy
CHEERLEADER	6. Former extra-curricular activity Izzy participated in
CLINGER	7. Mrs. Lingard describes Rosamunde as a ___.
ROMEO	8. The assignment for ___ & Juliet gives Izzy trouble.
MOTHER	9. A good ___ would stay.
CRUTCHES	10. Little Izzy did a back flip when Tony forgot to bring Izzy these.
JACK	11. Twin brother who does not visit Izzy in the hospital
BRAINS	12. According to Joel, Jack underestimates Izzy's.
SHOES	13. Mrs. Lingard removed all of Izzy's right ones from the closet.
HUMILIATED	14. How Izzy feels when she falls at school
SUZY	15. She calls Izzy to see if Izzy is going to tell that Marco had been drinking.
LEFT	16. The row of ___ shoes in the closet makes Rosamunde laugh.
TONY	17. He invites Izzy to join the newspaper staff
DORA	18. Dr. Epstein compares Izzy to this Dickens character
FRANCIE	19. Izzy's little sister
GRIGGERS	20. Marco's last name

Izzy, Willy-Nilly Matching 1

___ 1. LITTLE   A. What Izzy wants to give Rosamunde for Christmas
___ 2. TREE   B. Mrs. Hughes-Pincke, for example
___ 3. CRUTCHES   C. Mrs. Lingard describes Rosamunde as a ___.
___ 4. MARCO   D. He was responsible for the car accident.
___ 5. BRAINS   E. He invites Izzy to join the newspaper staff
___ 6. WEBBER   F. Dr. Epstein compares Izzy to this Dickens character
___ 7. LATIN   G. How Izzy feels when she falls at school
___ 8. LAUREN   H. Rosamunde's last name
___ 9. FRANCIE   I. Place to buy handmade crafts: ___ Trove
___10. CLINGER   J. A good ___ would stay.
___11. JOEL   K. Tony's girlfriend
___12. DORA   L. Lingards don't do this.
___13. LEFT   M. Izzy's little sister
___14. DEBORAH   N. Doctor who is Izzy's pediatrician
___15. DRUNK   O. The row of ___ shoes in the closet makes Rosamunde laugh.
___16. PIZZA   P. Twin brother who does visit Izzy
___17. TREASURE   Q. Little Izzy did a back flip when Tony forgot to bring Izzy these.
___18. THERAPIST   R. Object the car ran into
___19. TONY   S. Word describing Marco when he drove Izzy home
___20. HUMILIATED   T. According to Joel, Jack underestimates Izzy's.
___21. MOTHER   U. Izzy envisions ___ Izzy in her mind.
___22. EPSTEIN   V. Food Izzy wants to eat when she gets home
___23. ADELIA   W. Friend who avoids Izzy
___24. CRY   X. Club Izzy misses
___25. HAIRCUT   Y. Izzy's physical therapy nurse

Izzy, Willy-Nilly Matching 1 Answer Key

U - 1. LITTLE	A. What Izzy wants to give Rosamunde for Christmas
R - 2. TREE	B. Mrs. Hughes-Pincke, for example
Q - 3. CRUTCHES	C. Mrs. Lingard describes Rosamunde as a ___.
D - 4. MARCO	D. He was responsible for the car accident.
T - 5. BRAINS	E. He invites Izzy to join the newspaper staff
H - 6. WEBBER	F. Dr. Epstein compares Izzy to this Dickens character
X - 7. LATIN	G. How Izzy feels when she falls at school
W - 8. LAUREN	H. Rosamunde's last name
M - 9. FRANCIE	I. Place to buy handmade crafts: ___ Trove
C - 10. CLINGER	J. A good ___ would stay.
P - 11. JOEL	K. Tony's girlfriend
F - 12. DORA	L. Lingards don't do this.
O - 13. LEFT	M. Izzy's little sister
K - 14. DEBORAH	N. Doctor who is Izzy's pediatrician
S - 15. DRUNK	O. The row of ___ shoes in the closet makes Rosamunde laugh.
V - 16. PIZZA	P. Twin brother who does visit Izzy
I - 17. TREASURE	Q. Little Izzy did a back flip when Tony forgot to bring Izzy these.
B - 18. THERAPIST	R. Object the car ran into
E - 19. TONY	S. Word describing Marco when he drove Izzy home
G - 20. HUMILIATED	T. According to Joel, Jack underestimates Izzy's.
J - 21. MOTHER	U. Izzy envisions ___ Izzy in her mind.
N - 22. EPSTEIN	V. Food Izzy wants to eat when she gets home
Y - 23. ADELIA	W. Friend who avoids Izzy
L - 24. CRY	X. Club Izzy misses
A - 25. HAIRCUT	Y. Izzy's physical therapy nurse

Izzy, Willy-Nilly Matching 2

___ 1. LOOKS
___ 2. DRUNK
___ 3. FRANCIE
___ 4. POOL
___ 5. HAIRCUT
___ 6. MARCO
___ 7. CHEERLEADER
___ 8. DORA
___ 9. ADELIA
___ 10. HUMILIATED
___ 11. PIZZA
___ 12. EPSTEIN
___ 13. MOTHER
___ 14. TREE
___ 15. GRIGGERS
___ 16. ROMEO
___ 17. JOEL
___ 18. DEBORAH
___ 19. SHOES
___ 20. LATIN
___ 21. TONY
___ 22. CRUTCHES
___ 23. LINGARD
___ 24. SUZY
___ 25. BATIK

A. Tony's girlfriend
B. Twin brother who does visit Izzy
C. Dr. Epstein compares Izzy to this Dickens character
D. Marco's last name
E. Club Izzy misses
F. Word describing Marco when he drove Izzy home
G. Mrs. Lingard thinks Rosamunde must be uncomfortable because of the way she ___.
H. The assignment for ___ & Juliet gives Izzy trouble.
I. Little Izzy did a back flip when Tony forgot to bring Izzy these.
J. Doctor who is Izzy's pediatrician
K. Izzy's little sister
L. She calls Izzy to see if Izzy is going to tell that Marco had been drinking.
M. A good ___ would stay.
N. Izzy's last name
O. Mrs. Lingard removed all of Izzy's right ones from the closet.
P. Object the car ran into
Q. How Izzy feels when she falls at school
R. Rosamunde hangs an animal ___ on the hospital wall.
S. Food Izzy wants to eat when she gets home
T. He invites Izzy to join the newspaper staff
U. He was responsible for the car accident.
V. What Izzy wants to give Rosamunde for Christmas
W. Former extra-curricular activity Izzy participated in
X. Mr. Lingard wants to put one in the back yard
Y. Izzy's physical therapy nurse

Izzy, Willy-Nilly Matching 2 Answer Key

G - 1. LOOKS
F - 2. DRUNK
K - 3. FRANCIE
X - 4. POOL
V - 5. HAIRCUT
U - 6. MARCO
W - 7. CHEERLEADER
C - 8. DORA
Y - 9. ADELIA
Q -10. HUMILIATED
S -11. PIZZA
J -12. EPSTEIN
M -13. MOTHER
P -14. TREE
D -15. GRIGGERS
H -16. ROMEO
B -17. JOEL
A -18. DEBORAH
O -19. SHOES
E -20. LATIN
T -21. TONY
I -22. CRUTCHES
N -23. LINGARD
L -24. SUZY
R -25. BATIK

A. Tony's girlfriend
B. Twin brother who does visit Izzy
C. Dr. Epstein compares Izzy to this Dickens character
D. Marco's last name
E. Club Izzy misses
F. Word describing Marco when he drove Izzy home
G. Mrs. Lingard thinks Rosamunde must be uncomfortable because of the way she ___.
H. The assignment for ___ & Juliet gives Izzy trouble.
I. Little Izzy did a back flip when Tony forgot to bring Izzy these.
J. Doctor who is Izzy's pediatrician
K. Izzy's little sister
L. She calls Izzy to see if Izzy is going to tell that Marco had been drinking.
M. A good ___ would stay.
N. Izzy's last name
O. Mrs. Lingard removed all of Izzy's right ones from the closet.
P. Object the car ran into
Q. How Izzy feels when she falls at school
R. Rosamunde hangs an animal ___ on the hospital wall.
S. Food Izzy wants to eat when she gets home
T. He invites Izzy to join the newspaper staff
U. He was responsible for the car accident.
V. What Izzy wants to give Rosamunde for Christmas
W. Former extra-curricular activity Izzy participated in
X. Mr. Lingard wants to put one in the back yard
Y. Izzy's physical therapy nurse

Izzy, Willy-Nilly Matching 3

___ 1. SHOES   A. Izzy moves into her parents' on the first floor.
___ 2. DORA   B. Mrs. Lingard removed all of Izzy's right ones from the closet.
___ 3. CRY   C. Izzy's little sister
___ 4. FRANCIE   D. Tony's girlfriend
___ 5. EPSTEIN   E. Izzy's physical therapy nurse
___ 6. POOL   F. According to Joel, Jack underestimates Izzy's.
___ 7. TONY   G. Rosamunde hangs an animal ___ on the hospital wall.
___ 8. LEG   H. Lingards don't do this.
___ 9. DRUNK   I. He invites Izzy to join the newspaper staff
___10. MARCO   J. He was responsible for the car accident.
___11. CLINGER   K. Word describing Izzy
___12. ADELIA   L. Former extra-curricular activity Izzy participated in
___13. LATIN   M. Mrs. Lingard describes Rosamunde as a ___.
___14. LEFT   N. Half of Izzy's right one was amputated.
___15. BRAINS   O. What Izzy wants to give Rosamunde for Christmas
___16. BATIK   P. Mrs. Hughes-Pincke, for example
___17. ROMEO   Q. Club Izzy misses
___18. HAIRCUT   R. Mr. Lingard wants to put one in the back yard
___19. BEDROOM   S. The row of ___ shoes in the closet makes Rosamunde laugh.
___20. THERAPIST   T. The assignment for ___ & Juliet gives Izzy trouble.
___21. CHEERLEADER   U. Word describing Marco when he drove Izzy home
___22. TREE   V. Doctor who is Izzy's pediatrician
___23. DEBORAH   W. Food Izzy wants to eat when she gets home
___24. PIZZA   X. Dr. Epstein compares Izzy to this Dickens character
___25. NICE   Y. Object the car ran into

Izzy, Willy-Nilly Matching 3 Answer Key

B - 1. SHOES	A.	Izzy moves into her parents' ___ on the first floor.
X - 2. DORA	B.	Mrs. Lingard removed all of Izzy's right ones from the closet.
H - 3. CRY	C.	Izzy's little sister
C - 4. FRANCIE	D.	Tony's girlfriend
V - 5. EPSTEIN	E.	Izzy's physical therapy nurse
R - 6. POOL	F.	According to Joel, Jack underestimates Izzy's ___.
I - 7. TONY	G.	Rosamunde hangs an animal ___ on the hospital wall.
N - 8. LEG	H.	Lingards don't do this.
U - 9. DRUNK	I.	He invites Izzy to join the newspaper staff
J - 10. MARCO	J.	He was responsible for the car accident.
M - 11. CLINGER	K.	Word describing Izzy
E - 12. ADELIA	L.	Former extra-curricular activity Izzy participated in
Q - 13. LATIN	M.	Mrs. Lingard describes Rosamunde as a ___.
S - 14. LEFT	N.	Half of Izzy's right one was amputated.
F - 15. BRAINS	O.	What Izzy wants to give Rosamunde for Christmas
G - 16. BATIK	P.	Mrs. Hughes-Pincke, for example
T - 17. ROMEO	Q.	Club Izzy misses
O - 18. HAIRCUT	R.	Mr. Lingard wants to put one in the back yard
A - 19. BEDROOM	S.	The row of ___ shoes in the closet makes Rosamunde laugh.
P - 20. THERAPIST	T.	The assignment for ___ & Juliet gives Izzy trouble.
L - 21. CHEERLEADER	U.	Word describing Marco when he drove Izzy home
Y - 22. TREE	V.	Doctor who is Izzy's pediatrician
D - 23. DEBORAH	W.	Food Izzy wants to eat when she gets home
W - 24. PIZZA	X.	Dr. Epstein compares Izzy to this Dickens character
K - 25. NICE	Y.	Object the car ran into

Izzy, Willy-Nilly Matching 4

___ 1. BATIK   A. Rosamunde hangs an animal ___ on the hospital wall.
___ 2. WEBBER   B. Place to buy handmade crafts: ___ Trove
___ 3. GRIGGERS   C. Izzy moves into her parents' on the first floor.
___ 4. TONY   D. Twin brother who does not visit Izzy in the hospital
___ 5. TREASURE   E. According to Joel, Jack underestimates Izzy's.
___ 6. TREE   F. Rosamunde's last name
___ 7. THERAPIST   G. The row of ___ shoes in the closet makes Rosamunde laugh.
___ 8. FRANCIE   H. Game Izzy, her siblings, & Rosamunde play: ___ Pursuit
___ 9. JACK   I. Mrs. Lingard thinks Rosamunde must be uncomfortable because of the way she ___.
___ 10. CRUTCHES   J. Word describing Izzy
___ 11. SHOES   K. Mrs. Hughes-Pincke, for example
___ 12. MOTHER   L. Izzy's little sister
___ 13. LEG   M. Marco's last name
___ 14. CLINGER   N. He invites Izzy to join the newspaper staff
___ 15. HUMILIATED   O. Tony's girlfriend
___ 16. JEALOUS   P. How Izzy feels when she falls at school
___ 17. LEFT   Q. Object the car ran into
___ 18. LOOKS   R. Francie had been ___ of Izzy before the accident.
___ 19. PENS   S. Izzy wants to borrow Francie's
___ 20. DEBORAH   T. A good ___ would stay.
___ 21. BEDROOM   U. Mrs. Lingard removed all of Izzy's right ones from the closet.
___ 22. JOEL   V. Twin brother who does visit Izzy
___ 23. NICE   W. Mrs. Lingard describes Rosamunde as a ___.
___ 24. BRAINS   X. Little Izzy did a back flip when Tony forgot to bring Izzy these.
___ 25. TRIVIAL   Y. Half of Izzy's right one was amputated.

Izzy, Willy-Nilly Matching 4 Answer Key

A - 1. BATIK	A.	Rosamunde hangs an animal ___ on the hospital wall.
F - 2. WEBBER	B.	Place to buy handmade crafts: ___ Trove
M - 3. GRIGGERS	C.	Izzy moves into her parents' on the first floor.
N - 4. TONY	D.	Twin brother who does not visit Izzy in the hospital
B - 5. TREASURE	E.	According to Joel, Jack underestimates Izzy's.
Q - 6. TREE	F.	Rosamunde's last name
K - 7. THERAPIST	G.	The row of ___ shoes in the closet makes Rosamunde laugh.
L - 8. FRANCIE	H.	Game Izzy, her siblings, & Rosamunde play: ___ Pursuit
D - 9. JACK	I.	Mrs. Lingard thinks Rosamunde must be uncomfortable because of the way she ___.
X - 10. CRUTCHES	J.	Word describing Izzy
U - 11. SHOES	K.	Mrs. Hughes-Pincke, for example
T - 12. MOTHER	L.	Izzy's little sister
Y - 13. LEG	M.	Marco's last name
W - 14. CLINGER	N.	He invites Izzy to join the newspaper staff
P - 15. HUMILIATED	O.	Tony's girlfriend
R - 16. JEALOUS	P.	How Izzy feels when she falls at school
G - 17. LEFT	Q.	Object the car ran into
I - 18. LOOKS	R.	Francie had been ___ of Izzy before the accident.
S - 19. PENS	S.	Izzy wants to borrow Francie's
O - 20. DEBORAH	T.	A good ___ would stay.
C - 21. BEDROOM	U.	Mrs. Lingard removed all of Izzy's right ones from the closet.
V - 22. JOEL	V.	Twin brother who does visit Izzy
J - 23. NICE	W.	Mrs. Lingard describes Rosamunde as a ___.
E - 24. BRAINS	X.	Little Izzy did a back flip when Tony forgot to bring Izzy these.
H - 25. TRIVIAL	Y.	Half of Izzy's right one was amputated.

Izzy, Willy-Nilly Magic Squares 1

Match the definition with the vocabulary word. Put your answers in the magic squares below. When your answers are correct, all columns and rows will add to the same number.

A. LAUREN
B. WEBBER
C. LINGARD
D. MOTHER
E. BEDROOM
F. LITTLE
G. TREASURE
H. THERAPIST
I. JACK
J. PENS
K. CRUTCHES
L. PIZZA
M. CLINGER
N. TREE
O. GRIGGERS
P. ADELIA

1. Friend who avoids Izzy
2. Object the car ran into
3. Izzy wants to borrow Francie's
4. Izzy moves into her parents' ___ on the first floor.
5. Place to buy handmade crafts: ___ Trove
6. Food Izzy wants to eat when she gets home
7. Izzy's physical therapy nurse
8. Izzy's last name
9. Marco's last name
10. A good ___ would stay.
11. Mrs. Hughes-Pincke, for example
12. Little Izzy did a back flip when Tony forgot to bring Izzy these.
13. Twin brother who does not visit Izzy in the hospital
14. Izzy envisions ___ Izzy in her mind.
15. Rosamunde's last name
16. Mrs. Lingard describes Rosamunde as a ___.

A=	B=	C=	D=
E=	F=	G=	H=
I=	J=	K=	L=
M=	N=	O=	P=

Izzy, Willy-Nilly Magic Squares 1 Answer Key

Match the definition with the vocabulary word. Put your answers in the magic squares below. When your answers are correct, all columns and rows will add to the same number.

A. LAUREN
B. WEBBER
C. LINGARD
D. MOTHER
E. BEDROOM
F. LITTLE
G. TREASURE
H. THERAPIST
I. JACK
J. PENS
K. CRUTCHES
L. PIZZA
M. CLINGER
N. TREE
O. GRIGGERS
P. ADELIA

1. Friend who avoids Izzy
2. Object the car ran into
3. Izzy wants to borrow Francie's
4. Izzy moves into her parents' on the first floor.
5. Place to buy handmade crafts: ___ Trove
6. Food Izzy wants to eat when she gets home
7. Izzy's physical therapy nurse
8. Izzy's last name
9. Marco's last name
10. A good ___ would stay.
11. Mrs. Hughes-Pincke, for example
12. Little Izzy did a back flip when Tony forgot to bring Izzy these.
13. Twin brother who does not visit Izzy in the hospital
14. Izzy envisions ___ Izzy in her mind.
15. Rosamunde's last name
16. Mrs. Lingard describes Rosamunde as a ___.

A=1	B=15	C=8	D=10
E=4	F=14	G=5	H=11
I=13	J=3	K=12	L=6
M=16	N=2	O=9	P=7

Izzy, Willy-Nilly Magic Squares 2

Match the definition with the vocabulary word. Put your answers in the magic squares below. When your answers are correct, all columns and rows will add to the same number.

A. SHOES
B. LAUREN
C. FRANCIE
D. CRY
E. MOTHER
F. LITTLE
G. SUZY
H. WEBBER
I. ROSAMUNDE
J. HAIRCUT
K. CRUTCHES
L. ADELIA
M. TREE
N. JACK
O. THERAPIST
P. NICE

1. Object the car ran into
2. Izzy envisions ___ Izzy in her mind.
3. Rosamunde's last name
4. Mrs. Hughes-Pincke, for example
5. Izzy's physical therapy nurse
6. Izzy's little sister
7. Mrs. Lingard removed all of Izzy's right ones from the closet.
8. What Izzy wants to give Rosamunde for Christmas
9. Little Izzy did a back flip when Tony forgot to bring Izzy these.
10. Lingards don't do this.
11. Friend who avoids Izzy
12. Smart girl who becomes Izzy's friend
13. Twin brother who does not visit Izzy in the hospital
14. A good ___ would stay.
15. She calls Izzy to see if Izzy is going to tell that Marco had been drinking.
16. Word describing Izzy

A=	B=	C=	D=
E=	F=	G=	H=
I=	J=	K=	L=
M=	N=	O=	P=

Izzy, Willy-Nilly Magic Squares 2 Answer Key

Match the definition with the vocabulary word. Put your answers in the magic squares below. When your answers are correct, all columns and rows will add to the same number.

A. SHOES
B. LAUREN
C. FRANCIE
D. CRY
E. MOTHER
F. LITTLE
G. SUZY
H. WEBBER
I. ROSAMUNDE
J. HAIRCUT
K. CRUTCHES
L. ADELIA
M. TREE
N. JACK
O. THERAPIST
P. NICE

1. Object the car ran into
2. Izzy envisions ___ Izzy in her mind.
3. Rosamunde's last name
4. Mrs. Hughes-Pincke, for example
5. Izzy's physical therapy nurse
6. Izzy's little sister
7. Mrs. Lingard removed all of Izzy's right ones from the closet.
8. What Izzy wants to give Rosamunde for Christmas
9. Little Izzy did a back flip when Tony forgot to bring Izzy these.
10. Lingards don't do this.
11. Friend who avoids Izzy
12. Smart girl who becomes Izzy's friend
13. Twin brother who does not visit Izzy in the hospital
14. A good ___ would stay.
15. She calls Izzy to see if Izzy is going to tell that Marco had been drinking.
16. Word describing Izzy

A=7	B=11	C=6	D=10
E=14	F=2	G=15	H=3
I=12	J=8	K=9	L=5
M=1	N=13	O=4	P=16

Izzy, Willy-Nilly Magic Squares 3

Match the definition with the vocabulary word. Put your answers in the magic squares below. When your answers are correct, all columns and rows will add to the same number.

A. POOL
B. HAIRCUT
C. LEFT
D. TONY
E. FRANCIE
F. TREE
G. CRY
H. ADELIA
I. LAUREN
J. ROSAMUNDE
K. THERAPIST
L. SHOES
M. LOOKS
N. JOEL
O. LEG
P. WEBBER

1. Izzy's physical therapy nurse
2. Mrs. Lingard thinks Rosamunde must be uncomfortable because of the way she ___.
3. What Izzy wants to give Rosamunde for Christmas
4. Mrs. Hughes-Pincke, for example
5. Smart girl who becomes Izzy's friend
6. The row of ___ shoes in the closet makes Rosamunde laugh.
7. Rosamunde's last name
8. Izzy's little sister
9. Half of Izzy's right one was amputated.
10. Object the car ran into
11. Friend who avoids Izzy
12. He invites Izzy to join the newspaper staff
13. Mr. Lingard wants to put one in the back yard
14. Mrs. Lingard removed all of Izzy's right ones from the closet.
15. Lingards don't do this.
16. Twin brother who does visit Izzy

A=	B=	C=	D=
E=	F=	G=	H=
I=	J=	K=	L=
M=	N=	O=	P=

Izzy, Willy-Nilly Magic Squares 3 Answer Key

Match the definition with the vocabulary word. Put your answers in the magic squares below. When your answers are correct, all columns and rows will add to the same number.

A. POOL
B. HAIRCUT
C. LEFT
D. TONY
E. FRANCIE
F. TREE
G. CRY
H. ADELIA
I. LAUREN
J. ROSAMUNDE
K. THERAPIST
L. SHOES
M. LOOKS
N. JOEL
O. LEG
P. WEBBER

1. Izzy's physical therapy nurse
2. Mrs. Lingard thinks Rosamunde must be uncomfortable because of the way she ___.
3. What Izzy wants to give Rosamunde for Christmas
4. Mrs. Hughes-Pincke, for example
5. Smart girl who becomes Izzy's friend
6. The row of ___ shoes in the closet makes Rosamunde laugh.
7. Rosamunde's last name
8. Izzy's little sister
9. Half of Izzy's right one was amputated.
10. Object the car ran into
11. Friend who avoids Izzy
12. He invites Izzy to join the newspaper staff
13. Mr. Lingard wants to put one in the back yard
14. Mrs. Lingard removed all of Izzy's right ones from the closet.
15. Lingards don't do this.
16. Twin brother who does visit Izzy

A=13	B=3	C=6	D=12
E=8	F=10	G=15	H=1
I=11	J=5	K=4	L=14
M=2	N=16	O=9	P=7

Izzy, Willy-Nilly Magic Squares 4

Match the definition with the vocabulary word. Put your answers in the magic squares below. When your answers are correct, all columns and rows will add to the same number.

A. HUMILIATED
B. LEFT
C. POOL
D. DEBORAH
E. SHOES
F. GRIGGERS
G. LOOKS
H. THERAPIST
I. TRIVIAL
J. JEALOUS
K. DRUNK
L. CRY
M. CLINGER
N. NICE
O. JACK
P. LINGARD

1. Mrs. Hughes-Pincke, for example
2. How Izzy feels when she falls at school
3. The row of ___ shoes in the closet makes Rosamunde laugh.
4. Mrs. Lingard thinks Rosamunde must be uncomfortable because of the way she ___.
5. Francie had been ___ of Izzy before the accident.
6. Twin brother who does not visit Izzy in the hospital
7. Izzy's last name
8. Game Izzy, her siblings, & Rosamunde play: ___ Pursuit
9. Word describing Marco when he drove Izzy home
10. Word describing Izzy
11. Mrs. Lingard describes Rosamunde as a ___.
12. Lingards don't do this.
13. Mrs. Lingard removed all of Izzy's right ones from the closet.
14. Tony's girlfriend
15. Mr. Lingard wants to put one in the back yard
16. Marco's last name

A=	B=	C=	D=
E=	F=	G=	H=
I=	J=	K=	L=
M=	N=	O=	P=

Izzy, Willy-Nilly Magic Squares 4 Answer Key

Match the definition with the vocabulary word. Put your answers in the magic squares below. When your answers are correct, all columns and rows will add to the same number.

A. HUMILIATED
B. LEFT
C. POOL
D. DEBORAH
E. SHOES
F. GRIGGERS
G. LOOKS
H. THERAPIST
I. TRIVIAL
J. JEALOUS
K. DRUNK
L. CRY
M. CLINGER
N. NICE
O. JACK
P. LINGARD

1. Mrs. Hughes-Pincke, for example
2. How Izzy feels when she falls at school
3. The row of ___ shoes in the closet makes Rosamunde laugh.
4. Mrs. Lingard thinks Rosamunde must be uncomfortable because of the way she ___.
5. Francie had been ___ of Izzy before the accident.
6. Twin brother who does not visit Izzy in the hospital
7. Izzy's last name
8. Game Izzy, her siblings, & Rosamunde play: ___ Pursuit
9. Word describing Marco when he drove Izzy home
10. Word describing Izzy
11. Mrs. Lingard describes Rosamunde as a ___.
12. Lingards don't do this.
13. Mrs. Lingard removed all of Izzy's right ones from the closet.
14. Tony's girlfriend
15. Mr. Lingard wants to put one in the back yard
16. Marco's last name

A=2	B=3	C=15	D=14
E=13	F=16	G=4	H=1
I=8	J=5	K=9	L=12
M=11	N=10	O=6	P=7

Izzy, Willy-Nilly Word Search 1

```
L E O J M O T H E R W B A T I K G R H T
I E C B D X H R L J Z E P K B C E O S J
N G F J G A G S I F K K B O L D T S U W
G N J T R A W K L V N R C B A R M A Z W
A V L O I E Q K C U I R B E E T G M Y D
R P B L G P S S R L A A L E H R O U M J
D E E S G S B D U M I R L E L O L N Y S
D D H B E T L V T M E N R J R A I D B S
A V A S R E X H C E L A G D L Z T E H V
R B I Q S I W G H D P V E E J Y T I L D
M R R T Y N C C E I W B V M R F L F N S
C C C R M T C F S K B B H V R P E V K K
N K U E F F L T S G B B H A R T D H X V
T R T A B X H L L F R W N D S C K C P D
B R H S B T A L G C A C Q P U H D I V S
V H G U N U J R B K I B E K O P Z L W H
W K Q R R I A Q L E N N Y Y L Z O O T B
R O M E O T C R Y L S D O R A S H O E S
V F N B Z J K E M K R T H W E B N K L V
H U M I L I A T E D H L E G J Y W S D H
```

A good ___ would stay. (6)
According to Joel, Jack underestimates Izzy's. (6)
Club Izzy misses (5)
Doctor who is Izzy's pediatrician (7)
Dr. Epstein compares Izzy to this Dickens character (4)
Food Izzy wants to eat when she gets home (5)
Former extra-curricular activity Izzy participated in (11)
Francie had been ___ of Izzy before the accident. (7)
Friend who avoids Izzy (6)
Game Izzy, her siblings, & Rosamunde play: ___ Pursuit (7)
Half of Izzy's right one was amputated. (3)
He invites Izzy to join the newspaper staff (4)
He was responsible for the car accident. (5)
How Izzy feels when she falls at school (10)
Izzy envisions ___ Izzy in her mind. (6)
Izzy moves into her parents' on the first floor. (7)
Izzy wants to borrow Francie's (4)
Izzy's last name (7)
Izzy's little sister (7)
Izzy's physical therapy nurse (6)
Lingards don't do this. (3)
Little Izzy did a back flip when Tony forgot to bring Izzy these. (8)
Marco's last name (8)

Mr. Lingard wants to put one in the back yard (4)
Mrs. Hughes-Pincke, for example (9)
Mrs. Lingard describes Rosamunde as a ___. (7)
Mrs. Lingard removed all of Izzy's right ones from the closet. (5)
Mrs. Lingard thinks Rosamunde must be uncomfortable because of the way she ___. (5)
Object the car ran into (4)
Place to buy handmade crafts: ___ Trove (8)
Rosamunde hangs an animal ___ on the hospital wall. (5)
Rosamunde's last name (6)
She calls Izzy to see if Izzy is going to tell that Marco had been drinking. (4)
Smart girl who becomes Izzy's friend (9)
The assignment for ___ & Juliet gives Izzy trouble. (5)
The row of ___ shoes in the closet makes Rosamunde laugh. (4)
Tony's girlfriend (7)
Twin brother who does not visit Izzy in the hospital (4)
Twin brother who does visit Izzy (4)
What Izzy wants to give Rosamunde for Christmas (7)
Word describing Izzy (4)
Word describing Marco when he drove Izzy home (5)

Izzy, Willy-Nilly Word Search 1 Answer Key

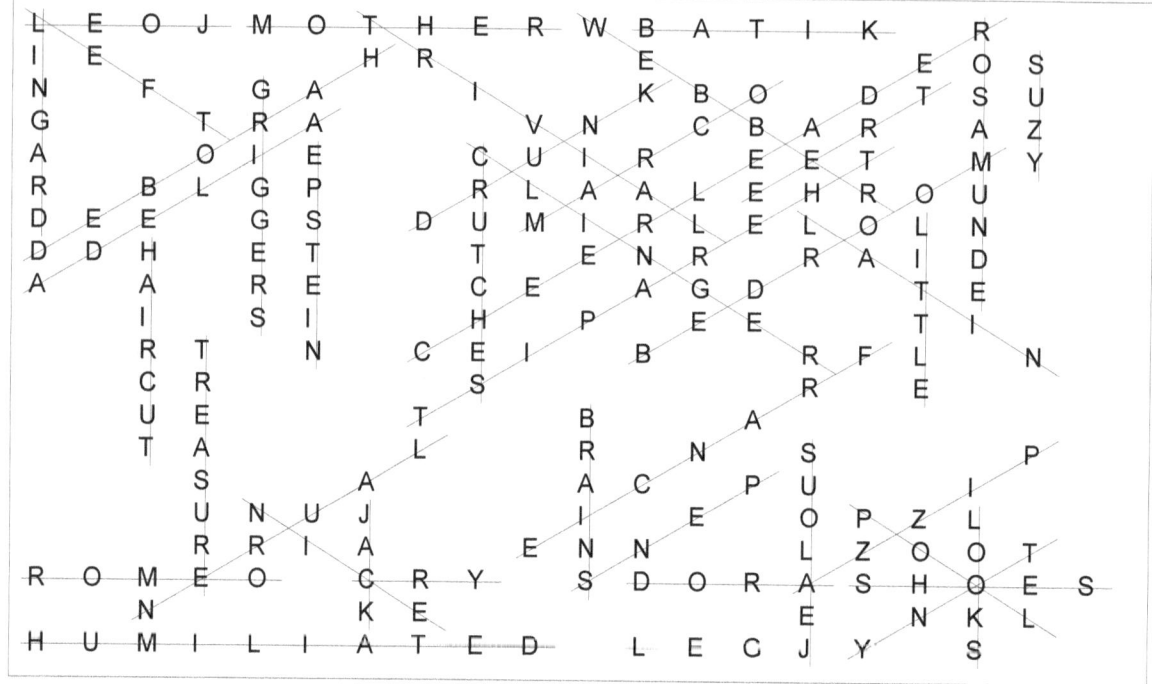

A good ___ would stay. (6)
According to Joel, Jack underestimates Izzy's. (6)
Club Izzy misses (5)
Doctor who is Izzy's pediatrician (7)
Dr. Epstein compares Izzy to this Dickens character (4)
Food Izzy wants to eat when she gets home (5)
Former extra-curricular activity Izzy participated in (11)
Francie had been ___ of Izzy before the accident. (7)
Friend who avoids Izzy (6)
Game Izzy, her siblings, & Rosamunde play: ___ Pursuit (7)
Half of Izzy's right one was amputated. (3)
He invites Izzy to join the newspaper staff (4)
He was responsible for the car accident. (5)
How Izzy feels when she falls at school (10)
Izzy envisions ___ Izzy in her mind. (6)
Izzy moves into her parents' on the first floor. (7)
Izzy wants to borrow Francie's (4)
Izzy's last name (7)
Izzy's little sister (7)
Izzy's physical therapy nurse (6)
Lingards don't do this. (3)
Little Izzy did a back flip when Tony forgot to bring Izzy these. (8)
Marco's last name (8)

Mr. Lingard wants to put one in the back yard (4)
Mrs. Hughes-Pincke, for example (9)
Mrs. Lingard describes Rosamunde as a ___. (7)
Mrs. Lingard removed all of Izzy's right ones from the closet. (5)
Mrs. Lingard thinks Rosamunde must be uncomfortable because of the way she ___. (5)
Object the car ran into (4)
Place to buy handmade crafts: ___ Trove (8)
Rosamunde hangs an animal ___ on the hospital wall. (5)
Rosamunde's last name (6)
She calls Izzy to see if Izzy is going to tell that Marco had been drinking. (4)
Smart girl who becomes Izzy's friend (9)
The assignment for ___ & Juliet gives Izzy trouble. (5)
The row of ___ shoes in the closet makes Rosamunde laugh. (4)
Tony's girlfriend (7)
Twin brother who does not visit Izzy in the hospital (4)
Twin brother who does visit Izzy (4)
What Izzy wants to give Rosamunde for Christmas (7)
Word describing Izzy (4)
Word describing Marco when he drove Izzy home (5)

Izzy, Willy-Nilly Word Search 2

```
G R I G G E R S M P K J M X T W R R L G
C Q B M D F M M V H P O T H D Z C B I W
L C X A T F D O X G O T Z F H Z E Y N L
H S T R T R W T R R T R H J R R C G G B
A Y R C T Z E H D M V G X C K A I K A C
I L E O J T H E R A P I S T P E N S R L
R L N R M N B R Q I O Q R C S U Z C D P
C Y A L O E W Q Z X O K L N R H D T I V
U H Y U K S O Z N B L I I D C P O R N E
T F E L R L A I V I R T C L I N G E R Q
P C T E P E E M Z C A A M T W W L A S H
R Q R L R T N G U L R B I H Q T L S K B
S Z M A S L J T Q N K U R N T Y Z U S Y
V W R P O F E X R M D E T I S R Q R T J
G O E O B V A A X P B E L C F C Z E A F
D Z K Y J C L M D B B V S L H X F I R D
G S N G Q G O H E E J A C K Y E L M C V
C K X D X K U W B Q R W N D W E S S T N
N W B J P D S P H Y Y T D J D B Z Z M Q
H U M I L I A T E D G D H A R O B E D C
```

A good ___ would stay. (6)
According to Joel, Jack underestimates Izzy's. (6)
Club Izzy misses (5)
Doctor who is Izzy's pediatrician (7)
Dr. Epstein compares Izzy to this Dickens character (4)
Food Izzy wants to eat when she gets home (5)
Former extra-curricular activity Izzy participated in (11)
Francie had been ___ of Izzy before the accident. (7)
Friend who avoids Izzy (6)
Game Izzy, her siblings, & Rosamunde play: ___ Pursuit (7)
Half of Izzy's right one was amputated. (3)
He invites Izzy to join the newspaper staff (4)
He was responsible for the car accident. (5)
How Izzy feels when she falls at school (10)
Izzy envisions ___ Izzy in her mind. (6)
Izzy moves into her parents' on the first floor. (7)
Izzy wants to borrow Francie's (4)
Izzy's last name (7)
Izzy's little sister (7)
Izzy's physical therapy nurse (6)
Lingards don't do this. (3)
Little Izzy did a back flip when Tony forgot to bring Izzy these. (8)
Marco's last name (8)

Mr. Lingard wants to put one in the back yard (4)
Mrs. Hughes-Pincke, for example (9)
Mrs. Lingard describes Rosamunde as a ___. (7)
Mrs. Lingard removed all of Izzy's right ones from the closet. (5)
Mrs. Lingard thinks Rosamunde must be uncomfortable because of the way she ___. (5)
Object the car ran into (4)
Place to buy handmade crafts: ___ Trove (8)
Rosamunde hangs an animal ___ on the hospital wall. (5)
Rosamunde's last name (6)
She calls Izzy to see if Izzy is going to tell that Marco had been drinking. (4)
Smart girl who becomes Izzy's friend (9)
The assignment for ___ & Juliet gives Izzy trouble. (5)
The row of ___ shoes in the closet makes Rosamunde laugh. (4)
Tony's girlfriend (7)
Twin brother who does not visit Izzy in the hospital (4)
Twin brother who does visit Izzy (4)
What Izzy wants to give Rosamunde for Christmas (7)
Word describing Izzy (4)
Word describing Marco when he drove Izzy home (5)

Izzy, Willy-Nilly Word Search 2 Answer Key

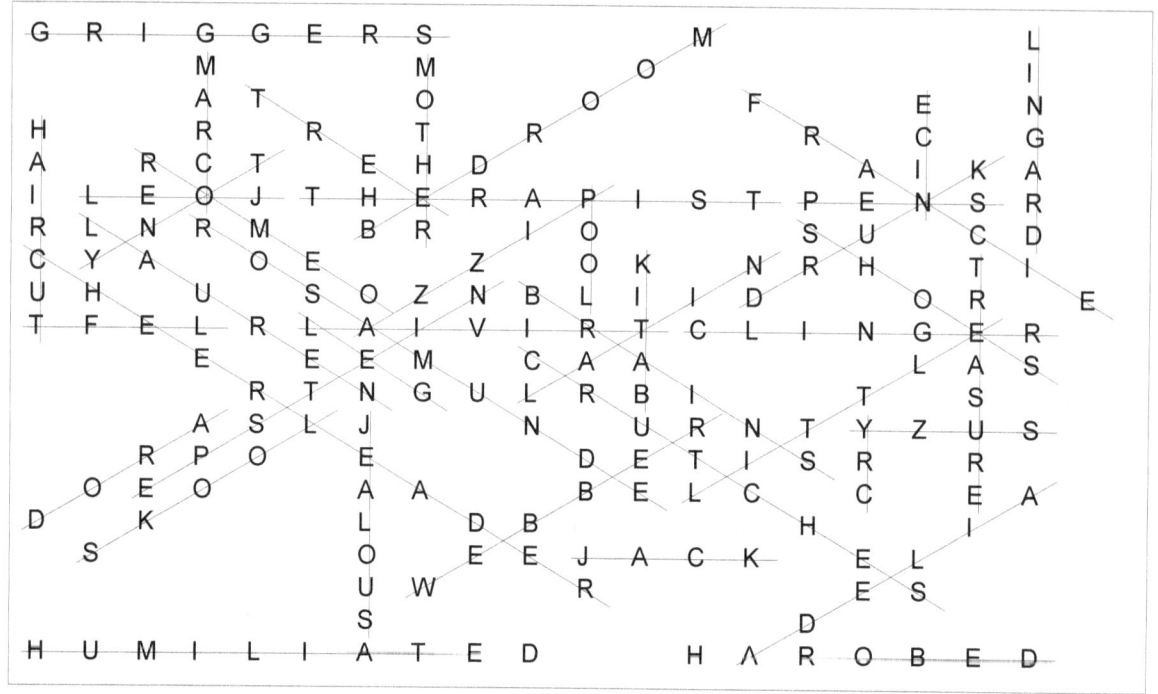

A good ___ would stay. (6)
According to Joel, Jack underestimates Izzy's. (6)
Club Izzy misses (5)
Doctor who is Izzy's pediatrician (7)
Dr. Epstein compares Izzy to this Dickens character (4)
Food Izzy wants to eat when she gets home (5)
Former extra-curricular activity Izzy participated in (11)
Francie had been ___ of Izzy before the accident. (7)
Friend who avoids Izzy (6)
Game Izzy, her siblings, & Rosamunde play: ___ Pursuit (7)
Half of Izzy's right one was amputated. (3)
He invites Izzy to join the newspaper staff (4)
He was responsible for the car accident. (5)
How Izzy feels when she falls at school (10)
Izzy envisions ___ Izzy in her mind. (6)
Izzy moves into her parents' on the first floor. (7)
Izzy wants to borrow Francie's (4)
Izzy's last name (7)
Izzy's little sister (7)
Izzy's physical therapy nurse (6)
Lingards don't do this. (3)
Little Izzy did a back flip when Tony forgot to bring Izzy these. (8)
Marco's last name (8)
Mr. Lingard wants to put one in the back yard (4)
Mrs. Hughes-Pincke, for example (9)
Mrs. Lingard describes Rosamunde as a ___. (7)
Mrs. Lingard removed all of Izzy's right ones from the closet. (5)
Mrs. Lingard thinks Rosamunde must be uncomfortable because of the way she ___. (5)
Object the car ran into (4)
Place to buy handmade crafts: ___ Trove (8)
Rosamunde hangs an animal ___ on the hospital wall. (5)
Rosamunde's last name (6)
She calls Izzy to see if Izzy is going to tell that Marco had been drinking. (4)
Smart girl who becomes Izzy's friend (9)
The assignment for ___ & Juliet gives Izzy trouble. (5)
The row of ___ shoes in the closet makes Rosamunde laugh. (4)
Tony's girlfriend (7)
Twin brother who does not visit Izzy in the hospital (4)
Twin brother who does visit Izzy (4)
What Izzy wants to give Rosamunde for Christmas (7)
Word describing Izzy (4)
Word describing Marco when he drove Izzy home (5)

Izzy, Willy-Nilly Word Search 3

```
T A D E L I A E Z B H A I R C U T Q H Q
H B C T J C Z P W E M D W K B F Q C U N
E A M V E H L S B D Z K J V H W M R M D
R T Y Q A E Z T R I V I A L F T M I K
A I Z R L E J E D O M M R G C S F Q L Y
P K P V O R R I H O V O W G D K N H I F
I Y T T U L Y N S M B W G W B W T A T
S K F C S E S H N E Y M L S Y T T Y T L
T X Z S Y A H J D W C J S D C P D S E H
T T B D W D K M W Q X D X J W V J K D F
P R R L W E S F V H C N X J B P Y Y K W
W E W J S R R M Y Q N L X Q H M L X P Z
M A L K V A N M G J D K I T J M I L N R
J S D B N Q X M S W R T W N S D N P N S
Y U K C D P L N D P U L L C G L G J P Q
Q R I G R E Y M P L N F A V X E A X Y L
L E G J T N R L O O K S E U M A R C O V
J J T R I S S T E D C E V M R O D O G L
S O Q T W T N M B Z R R T Y S E P F R B
B E A F E P O M R T S H U A W M N L I G
S L Z E B R Z K A R O D M T S O I B G X
C G Z L B B V Z I N S U D E C T C K G C
P F L W E G Z D N Q N U O Y T H E F E V
C R Y Y R I G X S D V H Z L L E E R R H
T O N Y P D G B E Q S Y E Y P R M S S F
```

ADELIA   DORA   JOEL   MOTHER   THERAPIST

BATIK   DRUNK   LATIN   NICE   TONY

BEDROOM   EPSTEIN   LAUREN   PENS   TREASURE

BRAINS   FRANCIE   LEFT   PIZZA   TREE

CHEERLEADER   GRIGGERS   LEG   POOL   TRIVIAL

CLINGER   HAIRCUT   LINGARD   ROMEO   WEBBER

CRUTCHES   HUMILIATED   LITTLE   ROSAMUNDE

CRY   JACK   LOOKS   SHOES

DEBORAH   JEALOUS   MARCO   SUZY

Izzy, Willy-Nilly Word Search 3 Answer Key

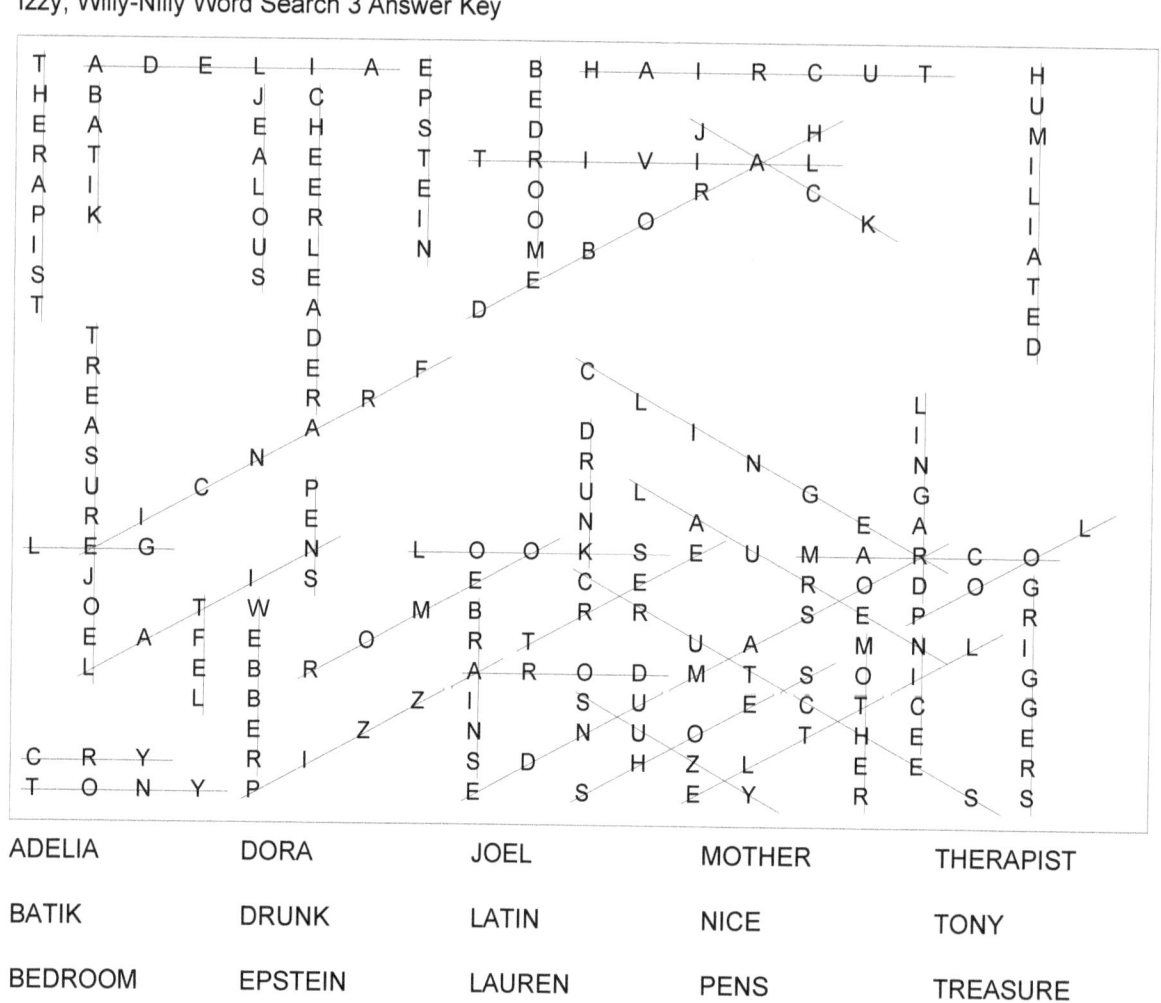

ADELIA	DORA	JOEL	MOTHER	THERAPIST
BATIK	DRUNK	LATIN	NICE	TONY
BEDROOM	EPSTEIN	LAUREN	PENS	TREASURE
BRAINS	FRANCIE	LEFT	PIZZA	TREE
CHEERLEADER	GRIGGERS	LEG	POOL	TRIVIAL
CLINGER	HAIRCUT	LINGARD	ROMEO	WEBBER
CRUTCHES	HUMILIATED	LITTLE	ROSAMUNDE	
CRY	JACK	LOOKS	SHOES	
DEBORAH	JEALOUS	MARCO	SUZY	

Izzy, Willy-Nilly Word Search 4

```
W D B D F Y H U M I L I A T E D G R C Z
J E F G C S S F Q M K P L N K H L H F F
J M B R H P G X V G B X Y T R L T M F Z
G R B B B C D N Z D G J P H L F R J N P
T D W W E S N L C N X M D E T Z E Q L Q
R G J T D R L Z F F K Y G R D M A W S D
X C Y G D B D R N S V Y F A S N S Y H Z
E Q G N C G C T R H S Q R P T D U Q O N
P N N L W R N D X B X K L I P R D E Z
S T J I Z N C R U T C H E S S N R P S V
T B C T F T Q A X M P N K T U I Q E C S
E V W T R A J G N T J O V Y C Z B Q H D
I Y D L D L P N K N O H O N R D Y Y E C
N I C E V J Y I L L N M A L L E O J E S
C J L Z B G B L Z B N R A A L E B T R P
L I K G S O Q Y S Z F S I R J B F M L Q
A A D T Y S R Y Y F A V B V C R J T E C
F Z T O N B R A R D I J A C K O E L A Y
Y L B I R C E H H R N H T L P S A A D W
W N A D N A H J T U Z A I I L A L U E Y
B R G L E G T J O N Y I K N Z M O R R L
B O G M L Z O H Z K N R H G P U U E N L
T M W T X H M H G G Y C N E B N S N R T
W E G R I G G E R S Y U W R F D C X F X
M O O R D E B H D Q X T G X L E Z K G G
```

ADELIA   DORA   JOEL   MOTHER   THERAPIST

BATIK   DRUNK   LATIN   NICE   TONY

BEDROOM   EPSTEIN   LAUREN   PENS   TREASURE

BRAINS   FRANCIE   LEFT   PIZZA   TREE

CHEERLEADER   GRIGGERS   LEG   POOL   TRIVIAL

CLINGER   HAIRCUT   LINGARD   ROMEO   WEBBER

CRUTCHES   HUMILIATED   LITTLE   ROSAMUNDE

CRY   JACK   LOOKS   SHOES

DEBORAH   JEALOUS   MARCO   SUZY

Izzy, Willy-Nilly Word Search 4 Answer Key

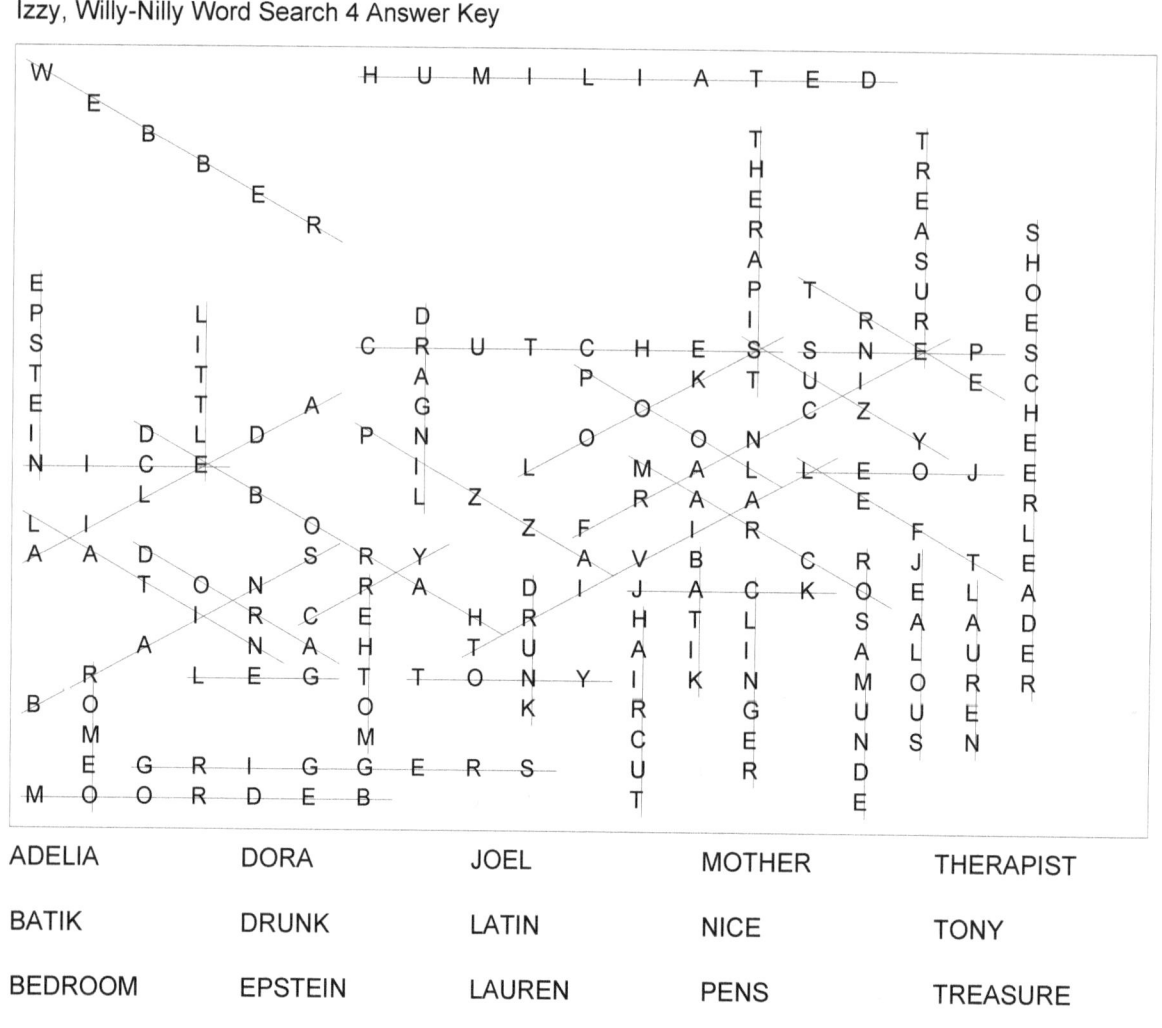

ADELIA	DORA	JOEL	MOTHER	THERAPIST
BATIK	DRUNK	LATIN	NICE	TONY
BEDROOM	EPSTEIN	LAUREN	PENS	TREASURE
BRAINS	FRANCIE	LEFT	PIZZA	TREE
CHEERLEADER	GRIGGERS	LEG	POOL	TRIVIAL
CLINGER	HAIRCUT	LINGARD	ROMEO	WEBBER
CRUTCHES	HUMILIATED	LITTLE	ROSAMUNDE	
CRY	JACK	LOOKS	SHOES	
DEBORAH	JEALOUS	MARCO	SUZY	

Izzy, Willy-Nilly Crossword 1

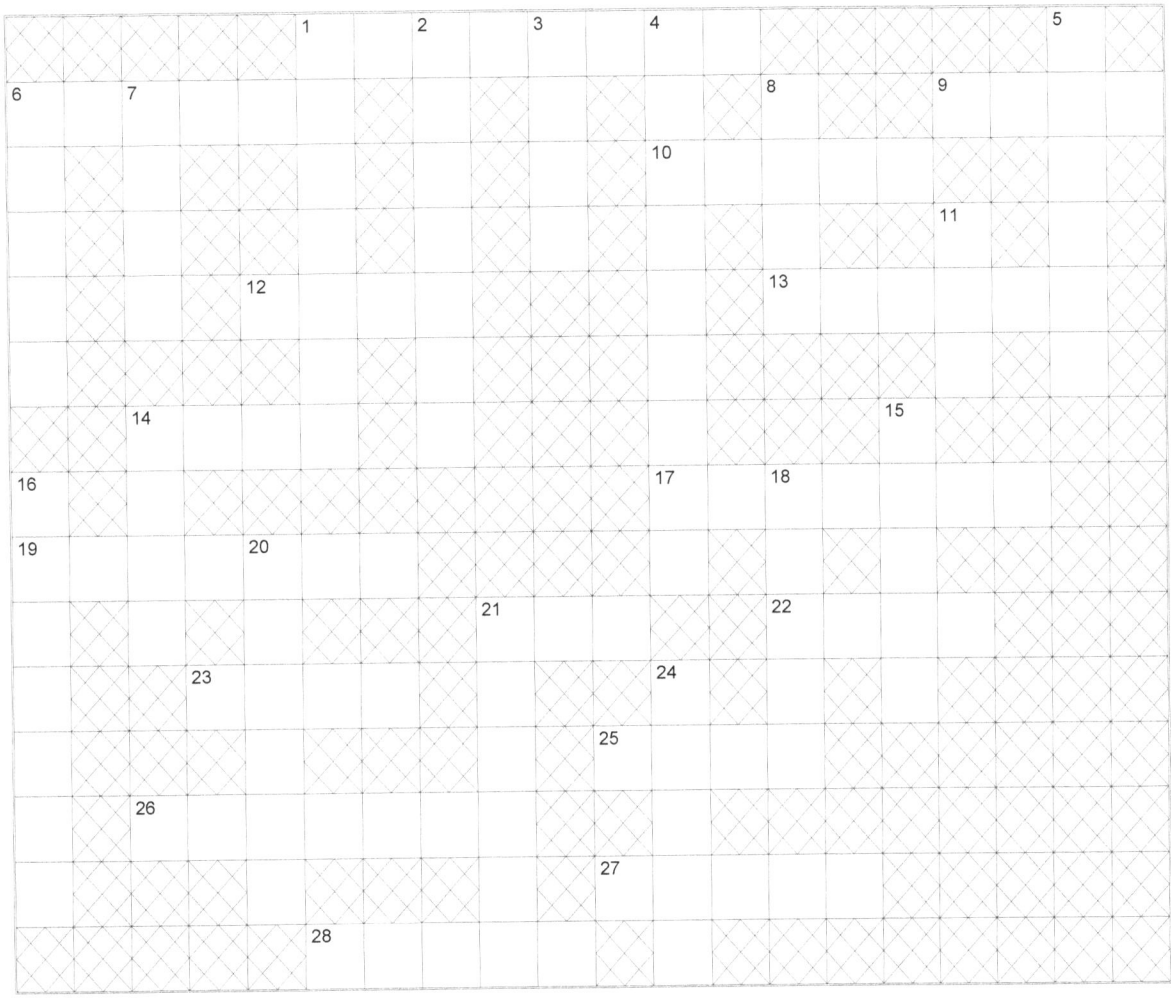

Across
1. Place to buy handmade crafts: ___ Trove
6. A good ___ would stay.
9. Dr. Epstein compares Izzy to this Dickens character
10. Mrs. Lingard removed all of Izzy's right ones from the closet.
12. Word describing Izzy
13. Friend who avoids Izzy
14. Mr. Lingard wants to put one in the back yard
17. Tony's girlfriend
19. Izzy's last name
21. Half of Izzy's right one was amputated.
22. He invites Izzy to join the newspaper staff
23. The row of ___ shoes in the closet makes Rosamunde laugh.
25. Twin brother who does not visit Izzy in the hospital
26. What Izzy wants to give Rosamunde for Christmas
27. Food Izzy wants to eat when she gets home
28. The assignment for ___ & Juliet gives Izzy trouble.

Down
1. Game Izzy, her siblings, & Rosamunde play: ___ Pursuit
2. Doctor who is Izzy's pediatrician
3. She calls Izzy to see if Izzy is going to tell that Marco had been drinking.
4. Smart girl who becomes Izzy's friend
5. According to Joel, Jack underestimates Izzy's.
6. He was responsible for the car accident.
7. Object the car ran into
8. Twin brother who does visit Izzy
11. Lingards don't do this.
14. Izzy wants to borrow Francie's
15. Word describing Marco when he drove Izzy home
16. Mrs. Lingard describes Rosamunde as a ___.
18. Rosamunde hangs an animal ___ on the hospital wall.
20. Izzy's physical therapy nurse
21. Izzy envisions ___ Izzy in her mind.
24. Club Izzy misses

Izzy, Willy-Nilly Crossword 1 Answer Key

				1 T	2 R	3 E A	S U	4 R E				5 B
6 M	O	7 T	H	E R	P		U	O	8 J		9 D O	R A
A		R		I	S		Z	10 S H	O	E S		A
R		E		V	T		Y	A		E		11 C I
C		E		12 N I	C E			M		13 L A	U R	E N
O				A		I		U			Y	S
		14 P	O	O L		N		N		15 D		
16 C		E						17 D E	18 B	O R A	H	
19 L	I	N	20 G	A R	D			E		A	U	
I		S		D			21 L	E G		22 T	O N	Y
N		23 L	E	F T		I			24 L	I	K	
G				L			25 T	J A	C	K		
E		26 H	A	I R	C	U T			T			
R				A				27 P I	Z	Z A		
				28 R	O	M	E	O	N			

Across
1. Place to buy handmade crafts: ___ Trove
6. A good ___ would stay.
9. Dr. Epstein compares Izzy to this Dickens character
10. Mrs. Lingard removed all of Izzy's right ones from the closet.
12. Word describing Izzy
13. Friend who avoids Izzy
14. Mr. Lingard wants to put one in the back yard
17. Tony's girlfriend
19. Izzy's last name
21. Half of Izzy's right one was amputated.
22. He invites Izzy to join the newspaper staff
23. The row of ___ shoes in the closet makes Rosamunde laugh.
25. Twin brother who does not visit Izzy in the hospital
26. What Izzy wants to give Rosamunde for Christmas
27. Food Izzy wants to eat when she gets home
28. The assignment for ___ & Juliet gives Izzy trouble.

Down
1. Game Izzy, her siblings, & Rosamunde play: ___ Pursuit
2. Doctor who is Izzy's pediatrician
3. She calls Izzy to see if Izzy is going to tell that Marco had been drinking.
4. Smart girl who becomes Izzy's friend
5. According to Joel, Jack underestimates Izzy's.
6. He was responsible for the car accident.
7. Object the car ran into
8. Twin brother who does visit Izzy
11. Lingards don't do this.
14. Izzy wants to borrow Francie's
15. Word describing Marco when he drove Izzy home
16. Mrs. Lingard describes Rosamunde as a ___.
18. Rosamunde hangs an animal ___ on the hospital wall.
20. Izzy's physical therapy nurse
21. Izzy envisions ___ Izzy in her mind.
24. Club Izzy misses

Izzy, Willy-Nilly Crossword 2

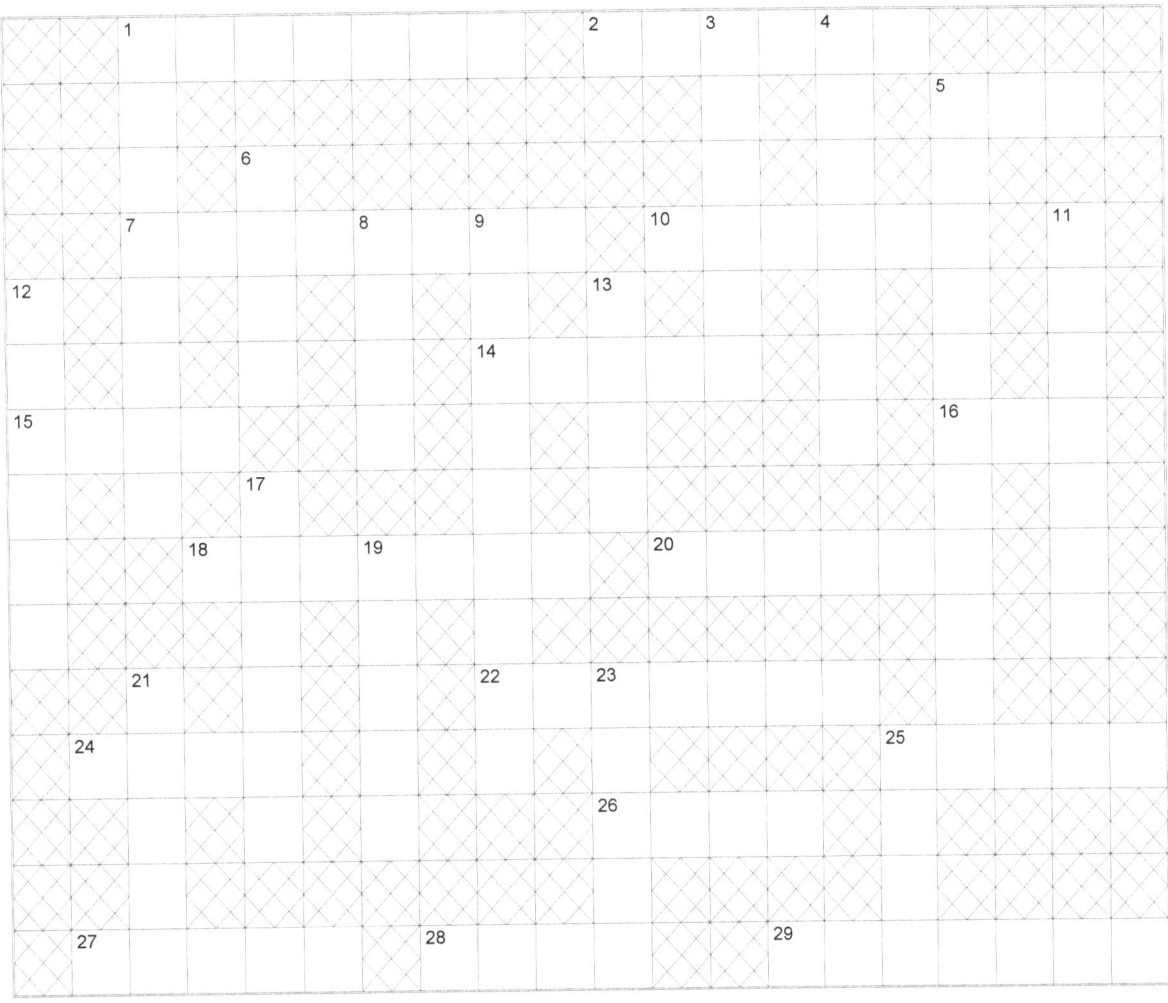

Across
1. Mrs. Lingard describes Rosamunde as a ___.
2. Rosamunde's last name
5. Lingards don't do this.
7. Place to buy handmade crafts: ___ Trove
10. Izzy envisions ___ Izzy in her mind.
14. Mrs. Lingard removed all of Izzy's right ones from the closet.
15. Object the car ran into
16. Half of Izzy's right one was amputated.
18. What Izzy wants to give Rosamunde for Christmas
20. Izzy's physical therapy nurse
22. Tony's girlfriend
24. Word describing Izzy
25. Word describing Marco when he drove Izzy home
26. He invites Izzy to join the newspaper staff
27. He was responsible for the car accident.
28. Twin brother who does not visit Izzy in the hospital
29. Francie had been ___ of Izzy before the accident.

Down
1. Little Izzy did a back flip when Tony forgot to bring Izzy these.
3. According to Joel, Jack underestimates Izzy's.
4. Doctor who is Izzy's pediatrician
5. Former extra-curricular activity Izzy participated in
6. The row of ___ shoes in the closet makes Rosamunde laugh.
8. She calls Izzy to see if Izzy is going to tell that Marco had been drinking.
9. Smart girl who becomes Izzy's friend
11. Izzy's last name
12. A good ___ would stay.
13. Twin brother who does visit Izzy
17. Friend who avoids Izzy
19. The assignment for ___ & Juliet gives Izzy trouble.
21. Food Izzy wants to eat when she gets home
23. Rosamunde hangs an animal ___ on the hospital wall.
25. Dr. Epstein compares Izzy to this Dickens character

Izzy, Willy-Nilly Crossword 2 Answer Key

	1 C	L	I	N	G	E	R		2 W	3 E	4 B	B	E	R		
	R									R	P			5 C	R	Y
	U		6 L							A	S			H		
	7 T	R	E	A	8 S	U	9 R	E		10 L	I	T	T	L	E	11 L
12 M		C		F		U		O		13 J		N	E	E		I
O		H		T		Z		14 S	H	O	E	S		I	R	N
15 T	R	E	E			Y		A		E				16 L	E	G
H		S		17 L				M		L				E		A
E			18 H	A	I	19 R	C	U	T		20 A	D	E	L	I	A
R			U			O		N						A		R
		21 P	R			M		22 D	E	23 B	O	R	A	H		
	24 N	I	C	E		E		E		A				25 D	R	U	N	K
		Z		N		O				26 T	O	N	Y		O	
		Z								I					R	
	27 M	A	R	C	O		28 J	A	C	K		29 J	E	A	L	O	U	S

Across
1. Mrs. Lingard describes Rosamunde as a ___.
2. Rosamunde's last name
5. Lingards don't do this.
7. Place to buy handmade crafts: ___ Trove
10. Izzy envisions ___ Izzy in her mind.
14. Mrs. Lingard removed all of Izzy's right ones from the closet.
15. Object the car ran into
16. Half of Izzy's right one was amputated.
18. What Izzy wants to give Rosamunde for Christmas
20. Izzy's physical therapy nurse
22. Tony's girlfriend
24. Word describing Izzy
25. Word describing Marco when he drove Izzy home
26. He invites Izzy to join the newspaper staff
27. He was responsible for the car accident.
28. Twin brother who does not visit Izzy in the hospital
29. Francie had been ___ of Izzy before the accident.

Down
1. Little Izzy did a back flip when Tony forgot to bring Izzy these.
3. According to Joel, Jack underestimates Izzy's.
4. Doctor who is Izzy's pediatrician
5. Former extra-curricular activity Izzy participated in
6. The row of ___ shoes in the closet makes Rosamunde laugh.
8. She calls Izzy to see if Izzy is going to tell that Marco had been drinking.
9. Smart girl who becomes Izzy's friend
11. Izzy's last name
12. A good ___ would stay.
13. Twin brother who does visit Izzy
17. Friend who avoids Izzy
19. The assignment for ___ & Juliet gives Izzy trouble.
21. Food Izzy wants to eat when she gets home
23. Rosamunde hangs an animal ___ on the hospital wall.
25. Dr. Epstein compares Izzy to this Dickens character

Izzy, Willy-Nilly Crossword 3

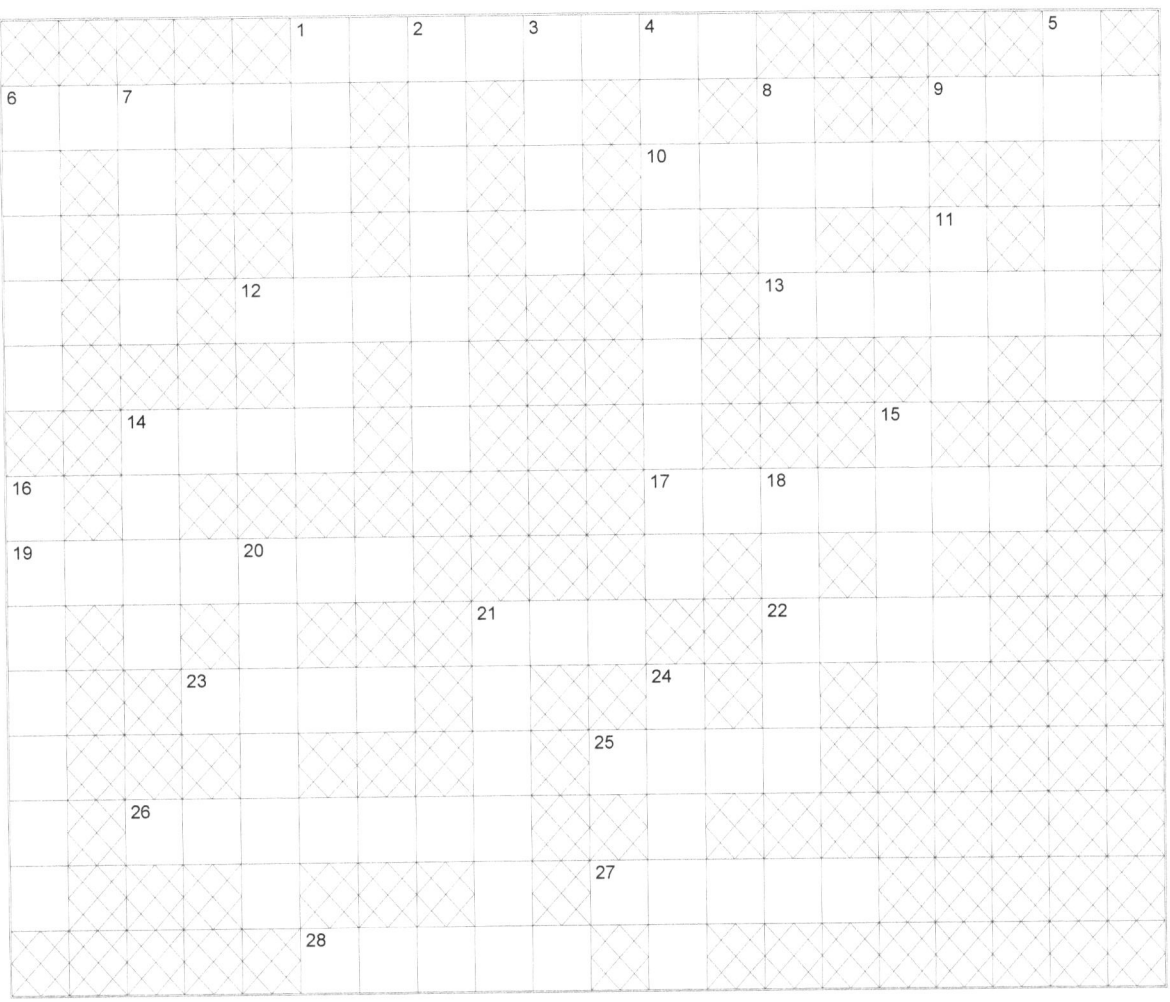

Across
1. Place to buy handmade crafts: ___ Trove
6. A good ___ would stay.
9. Dr. Epstein compares Izzy to this Dickens character
10. Mrs. Lingard removed all of Izzy's right ones from the closet.
12. Word describing Izzy
13. Friend who avoids Izzy
14. Mr. Lingard wants to put one in the back yard
17. Tony's girlfriend
19. Izzy's last name
21. Half of Izzy's right one was amputated.
22. He invites Izzy to join the newspaper staff
23. The row of ___ shoes in the closet makes Rosamunde laugh.
25. Twin brother who does not visit Izzy in the hospital
26. What Izzy wants to give Rosamunde for Christmas
27. Food Izzy wants to eat when she gets home
28. The assignment for ___ & Juliet gives Izzy trouble.

Down
1. Game Izzy, her siblings, & Rosamunde play: ___ Pursuit
2. Doctor who is Izzy's pediatrician
3. She calls Izzy to see if Izzy is going to tell that Marco had been drinking.
4. Smart girl who becomes Izzy's friend
5. According to Joel, Jack underestimates Izzy's.
6. He was responsible for the car accident.
7. Object the car ran into
8. Twin brother who does visit Izzy
11. Lingards don't do this.
14. Izzy wants to borrow Francie's
15. Word describing Marco when he drove Izzy home
16. Mrs. Lingard describes Rosamunde as a ___.
18. Rosamunde hangs an animal ___ on the hospital wall.
20. Izzy's physical therapy nurse
21. Izzy envisions ___ Izzy in her mind.
24. Club Izzy misses

Izzy, Willy-Nilly Crossword 3 Answer Key

				1 T	2 R	3 E	A	S	4 U	R	E				5 B
6 M	O	7 T	H	E	R	P		U	O			8 J		9 D	O	R	A
A		R		I		S		Z	10 S	H	O	E	S		A
R		E		V		T		Y	A			E		11 C		I
C		E		12 N	I	C	E		M			13 L	A	U	R	E	N
O				A		I			U			15 D		Y		S
		14 P	O	O	L	N			N						
16 C		E							17 D	18 E	B	O	R	A	H
19 L	I	20 N	G	A	R	D			E	A			U		
I		S				21 L	E	G		22 T	O	N	Y		
23 N		L	E	F	T	I			24 L	I	K			
G		L				T	25 J	A	C	K				
E		26 H	A	I	R	C	U	T	T					
R		A					27 P	I	Z	Z	A			
		28 R	O	M	E	O		N						

Across
1. Place to buy handmade crafts: ___ Trove
6. A good ___ would stay.
9. Dr. Epstein compares Izzy to this Dickens character
10. Mrs. Lingard removed all of Izzy's right ones from the closet.
12. Word describing Izzy
13. Friend who avoids Izzy
14. Mr. Lingard wants to put one in the back yard
17. Tony's girlfriend
19. Izzy's last name
21. Half of Izzy's right one was amputated.
22. He invites Izzy to join the newspaper staff
23. The row of ___ shoes in the closet makes Rosamunde laugh.
25. Twin brother who does not visit Izzy in the hospital
26. What Izzy wants to give Rosamunde for Christmas
27. Food Izzy wants to eat when she gets home
28. The assignment for ___ & Juliet gives Izzy trouble.

Down
1. Game Izzy, her siblings, & Rosamunde play: ___ Pursuit
2. Doctor who is Izzy's pediatrician
3. She calls Izzy to see if Izzy is going to tell that Marco had been drinking.
4. Smart girl who becomes Izzy's friend
5. According to Joel, Jack underestimates Izzy's.
6. He was responsible for the car accident.
7. Object the car ran into
8. Twin brother who does visit Izzy
11. Lingards don't do this.
14. Izzy wants to borrow Francie's
15. Word describing Marco when he drove Izzy home
16. Mrs. Lingard describes Rosamunde as a ___.
18. Rosamunde hangs an animal ___ on the hospital wall.
20. Izzy's physical therapy nurse
21. Izzy envisions ___ Izzy in her mind.
24. Club Izzy misses

Izzy, Willy-Nilly Crossword 4

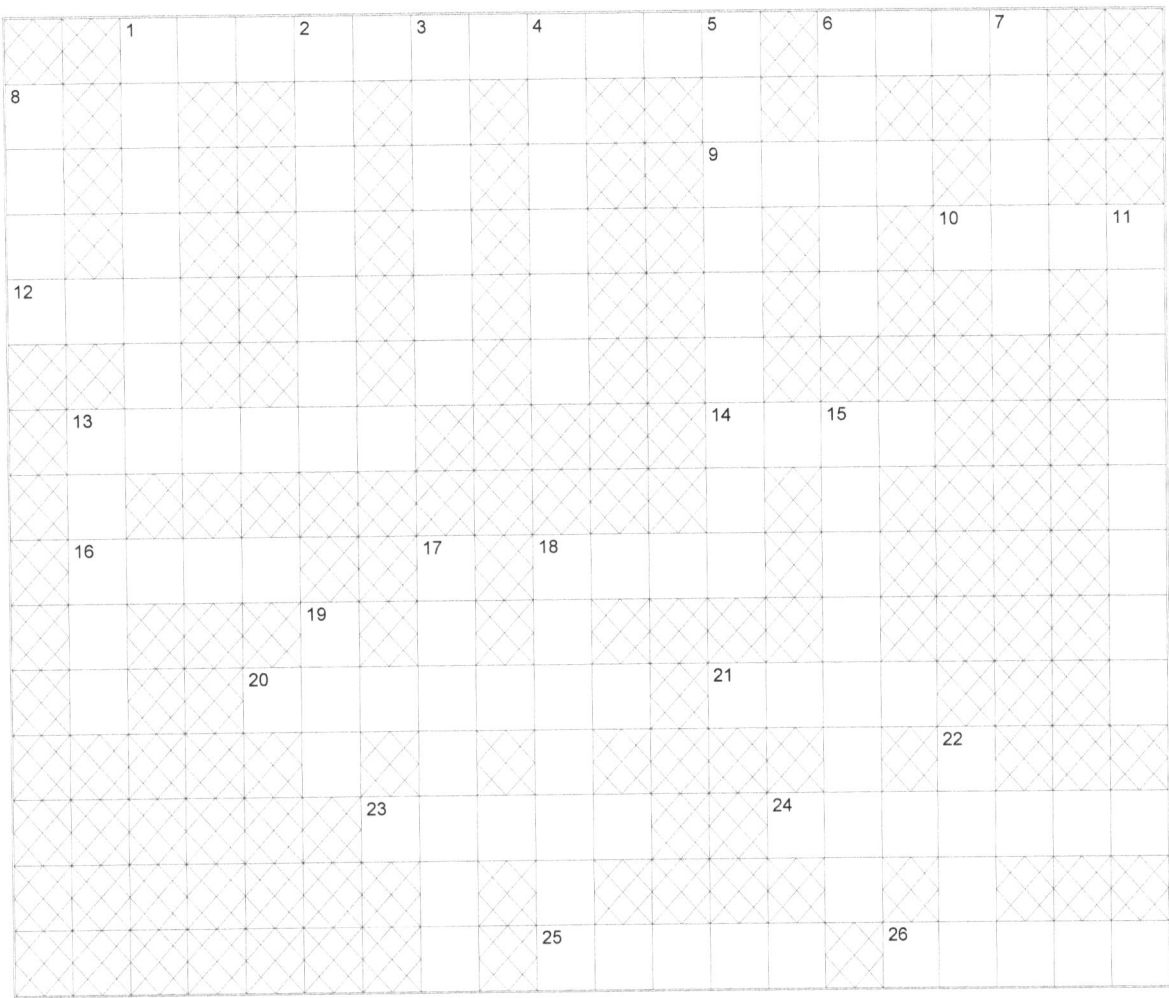

Across
1. Former extra-curricular activity Izzy participated in
6. Izzy wants to borrow Francie's ___
9. She calls Izzy to see if Izzy is going to tell that Marco had been drinking.
10. The row of ___ shoes in the closet makes Rosamunde laugh.
12. Half of Izzy's right one was amputated.
13. According to Joel, Jack underestimates Izzy's ___.
14. Word describing Izzy
16. He invites Izzy to join the newspaper staff
18. Object the car ran into
20. Izzy's little sister
21. Twin brother who does not visit Izzy in the hospital
23. Club Izzy misses
24. Tony's girlfriend
25. Mrs. Lingard thinks Rosamunde must be uncomfortable because of the way she ___.
26. He was responsible for the car accident.

Down
1. Mrs. Lingard describes Rosamunde as a ___.
2. Doctor who is Izzy's pediatrician
3. Friend who avoids Izzy
4. Izzy's physical therapy nurse
5. Smart girl who becomes Izzy's friend
6. Food Izzy wants to eat when she gets home
7. Mrs. Lingard removed all of Izzy's right ones from the closet.
8. Twin brother who does visit Izzy
11. Place to buy handmade crafts: ___ Trove
13. Rosamunde hangs an animal ___ on the hospital wall.
15. Little Izzy did a back flip when Tony forgot to bring Izzy these.
17. Izzy's last name
18. Game Izzy, her siblings, & Rosamunde play: ___ Pursuit
19. Lingards don't do this.
22. Dr. Epstein compares Izzy to this Dickens character

Izzy, Willy-Nilly Crossword 4 Answer Key

	1 C	H	2 E	3 R	4 L	E	A	D	5 E	R		6 P	E	N	7 S
8 J		L		P	A	D			O			I			H
O		I		S	U	E		9 S	U	Z	Y				O
E		N		T	R	L		A		Z		10 L	E	F	11 T
12 L	E	G		E	E	I		M		A		S			R
		E		I	N	A		U							E
	13 B	R	A	I	N	S			14 N	I	15 C	E			A
	A								D		R				S
	16 T	O	N	Y		17 L	18 T	R	E	E		U			U
	I			19 C		I	R					T			R
	K		20 F	R	A	N	C	I	E		21 J	A	C	K	E
				Y		G	V				H		22 D		
				23 L	A	T	I	N		24 D	E	B	O	R	A H
				R			A			S			R		
				25 D		L	O	O	K	S		26 M	A	R	C O

Across
1. Former extra-curricular activity Izzy participated in
6. Izzy wants to borrow Francie's
9. She calls Izzy to see if Izzy is going to tell that Marco had been drinking.
10. The row of ___ shoes in the closet makes Rosamunde laugh.
12. Half of Izzy's right one was amputated.
13. According to Joel, Jack underestimates Izzy's.
14. Word describing Izzy
16. He invites Izzy to join the newspaper staff
18. Object the car ran into
20. Izzy's little sister
21. Twin brother who does not visit Izzy in the hospital
23. Club Izzy misses
24. Tony's girlfriend
25. Mrs. Lingard thinks Rosamunde must be uncomfortable because of the way she ___.
26. He was responsible for the car accident.

Down
1. Mrs. Lingard describes Rosamunde as a ___.
2. Doctor who is Izzy's pediatrician
3. Friend who avoids Izzy
4. Izzy's physical therapy nurse
5. Smart girl who becomes Izzy's friend
6. Food Izzy wants to eat when she gets home
7. Mrs. Lingard removed all of Izzy's right ones from the closet.
8. Twin brother who does visit Izzy
11. Place to buy handmade crafts: ___ Trove
13. Rosamunde hangs an animal ___ on the hospital wall.
15. Little Izzy did a back flip when Tony forgot to bring Izzy these.
17. Izzy's last name
18. Game Izzy, her siblings, & Rosamunde play: ___ Pursuit
19. Lingards don't do this.
22. Dr. Epstein compares Izzy to this Dickens character

Izzy, Willy-Nilly

DRUNK	TREASURE	LITTLE	PIZZA	CRUTCHES
CRY	FRANCIE	TONY	EPSTEIN	JACK
LOOKS	BEDROOM	FREE SPACE	ROMEO	TRIVIAL
MARCO	ADELIA	NICE	CLINGER	PENS
HUMILIATED	SUZY	THERAPIST	CHEERLEADER	TREE

Izzy, Willy-Nilly

LEFT	GRIGGERS	POOL	MOTHER	JEALOUS
LAUREN	LATIN	JOEL	DEBORAH	SHOES
HAIRCUT	WEBBER	FREE SPACE	LEG	BATIK
DORA	LINGARD	TREE	CHEERLEADER	THERAPIST
SUZY	HUMILIATED	PENS	CLINGER	NICE

Izzy, Willy-Nilly

MOTHER	LINGARD	TREASURE	CRY	JEALOUS
BEDROOM	TREE	ADELIA	CRUTCHES	LATIN
FRANCIE	DRUNK	FREE SPACE	HUMILIATED	LEFT
EPSTEIN	THERAPIST	PIZZA	GRIGGERS	CLINGER
TRIVIAL	ROMEO	SHOES	NICE	WEBBER

Izzy, Willy-Nilly

TONY	HAIRCUT	POOL	LOOKS	LAUREN
DEBORAH	JACK	LEG	BATIK	DORA
JOEL	PENS	FREE SPACE	MARCO	ROSAMUNDE
CHEERLEADER	BRAINS	WEBBER	NICE	SHOES
ROMEO	TRIVIAL	CLINGER	GRIGGERS	PIZZA

Izzy, Willy-Nilly

LEG	FRANCIE	LOOKS	BATIK	LAUREN
NICE	GRIGGERS	PIZZA	BRAINS	JOEL
LATIN	DORA	FREE SPACE	ROSAMUNDE	MARCO
LEFT	TRIVIAL	JEALOUS	POOL	DEBORAH
CRY	TREE	DRUNK	ADELIA	HUMILIATED

Izzy, Willy-Nilly

CHEERLEADER	CRUTCHES	PENS	BEDROOM	TONY
HAIRCUT	MOTHER	SUZY	LITTLE	TREASURE
THERAPIST	CLINGER	FREE SPACE	JACK	ROMEO
EPSTEIN	LINGARD	HUMILIATED	ADELIA	DRUNK
TREE	CRY	DEBORAH	POOL	JEALOUS

Izzy, Willy-Nilly

WEBBER	GRIGGERS	JACK	ROSAMUNDE	LAUREN
ROMEO	DRUNK	JOEL	CRY	FRANCIE
JEALOUS	TONY	FREE SPACE	LINGARD	SHOES
THERAPIST	LEFT	MOTHER	TREE	CLINGER
PIZZA	TRIVIAL	MARCO	BRAINS	LOOKS

Izzy, Willy-Nilly

BATIK	HUMILIATED	DORA	BEDROOM	DEBORAH
PENS	LEG	ADELIA	EPSTEIN	LITTLE
TREASURE	POOL	FREE SPACE	SUZY	HAIRCUT
LATIN	CHEERLEADER	LOOKS	BRAINS	MARCO
TRIVIAL	PIZZA	CLINGER	TREE	MOTHER

Izzy, Willy-Nilly

NICE	TREE	SHOES	PENS	THERAPIST
CRUTCHES	ROSAMUNDE	LITTLE	LAUREN	JACK
TONY	FRANCIE	FREE SPACE	DRUNK	WEBBER
JOEL	LEFT	HUMILIATED	ADELIA	TREASURE
BRAINS	PIZZA	ROMEO	MARCO	GRIGGERS

Izzy, Willy-Nilly

TRIVIAL	JEALOUS	LATIN	HAIRCUT	SUZY
CHEERLEADER	BATIK	LOOKS	MOTHER	LEG
EPSTEIN	LINGARD	FREE SPACE	DORA	POOL
DEBORAH	CRY	GRIGGERS	MARCO	ROMEO
PIZZA	BRAINS	TREASURE	ADELIA	HUMILIATED

Izzy, Willy-Nilly

POOL	TREE	LINGARD	EPSTEIN	LAUREN
ROSAMUNDE	FRANCIE	BATIK	MARCO	JACK
GRIGGERS	PENS	FREE SPACE	DORA	THERAPIST
CRY	TONY	LITTLE	DRUNK	CHEERLEADER
BEDROOM	PIZZA	HUMILIATED	LEG	HAIRCUT

Izzy, Willy-Nilly

NICE	LATIN	CRUTCHES	TREASURE	BRAINS
JOEL	SUZY	LOOKS	ADELIA	LEFT
WEBBER	CLINGER	FREE SPACE	DEBORAH	TRIVIAL
ROMEO	SHOES	HAIRCUT	LEG	HUMILIATED
PIZZA	BEDROOM	CHEERLEADER	DRUNK	LITTLE

Izzy, Willy-Nilly

CLINGER	LEFT	TRIVIAL	BRAINS	LITTLE
ROMEO	CHEERLEADER	TREE	LOOKS	MARCO
DORA	WEBBER	FREE SPACE	JACK	NICE
CRUTCHES	ADELIA	SUZY	MOTHER	BATIK
POOL	LINGARD	FRANCIE	BEDROOM	EPSTEIN

Izzy, Willy-Nilly

GRIGGERS	HAIRCUT	TREASURE	PIZZA	LATIN
CRY	ROSAMUNDE	LAUREN	HUMILIATED	PENS
LEG	THERAPIST	FREE SPACE	DRUNK	JOEL
DEBORAH	TONY	EPSTEIN	BEDROOM	FRANCIE
LINGARD	POOL	BATIK	MOTHER	SUZY

Izzy, Willy-Nilly

DEBORAH	WEBBER	LAUREN	ROMEO	LATIN
ROSAMUNDE	HAIRCUT	CRY	HUMILIATED	SUZY
LINGARD	EPSTEIN	FREE SPACE	LEG	TREASURE
SHOES	THERAPIST	BEDROOM	LITTLE	LOOKS
PENS	CHEERLEADER	TRIVIAL	BATIK	ADELIA

Izzy, Willy-Nilly

CLINGER	DRUNK	LEFT	PIZZA	BRAINS
JACK	NICE	FRANCIE	POOL	DORA
JEALOUS	JOEL	FREE SPACE	CRUTCHES	TONY
MARCO	TREE	ADELIA	BATIK	TRIVIAL
CHEERLEADER	PENS	LOOKS	LITTLE	BEDROOM

Izzy, Willy-Nilly

PIZZA	ROMEO	TREASURE	WEBBER	NICE
CRUTCHES	DEBORAH	PENS	LATIN	HAIRCUT
LEG	SUZY	FREE SPACE	JACK	ADELIA
TREE	LOOKS	POOL	THERAPIST	GRIGGERS
MARCO	BATIK	LAUREN	EPSTEIN	LEFT

Izzy, Willy-Nilly

CHEERLEADER	SHOES	MOTHER	CLINGER	BRAINS
TRIVIAL	HUMILIATED	ROSAMUNDE	DRUNK	CRY
LINGARD	JOEL	FREE SPACE	BEDROOM	JEALOUS
LITTLE	FRANCIE	LEFT	EPSTEIN	LAUREN
BATIK	MARCO	GRIGGERS	THERAPIST	POOL

Izzy, Willy-Nilly

LITTLE	LEG	GRIGGERS	NICE	WEBBER
DEBORAH	BEDROOM	TRIVIAL	BRAINS	BATIK
LINGARD	HUMILIATED	FREE SPACE	ADELIA	ROMEO
TONY	JACK	MARCO	POOL	CLINGER
TREE	CRY	TREASURE	LAUREN	JEALOUS

Izzy, Willy-Nilly

CRUTCHES	SHOES	MOTHER	JOEL	DORA
PENS	CHEERLEADER	PIZZA	FRANCIE	SUZY
THERAPIST	LATIN	FREE SPACE	LOOKS	LEFT
DRUNK	EPSTEIN	JEALOUS	LAUREN	TREASURE
CRY	TREE	CLINGER	POOL	MARCO

Izzy, Willy-Nilly

DEBORAH	DRUNK	LEG	TREE	LITTLE
ROMEO	MARCO	JOEL	PENS	BEDROOM
WEBBER	JEALOUS	FREE SPACE	LEFT	MOTHER
JACK	CRUTCHES	CHEERLEADER	LAUREN	POOL
THERAPIST	EPSTEIN	LATIN	FRANCIE	ROSAMUNDE

Izzy, Willy-Nilly

PIZZA	SHOES	NICE	LINGARD	BATIK
HAIRCUT	TRIVIAL	CRY	BRAINS	LOOKS
TREASURE	DORA	FREE SPACE	CLINGER	TONY
GRIGGERS	HUMILIATED	ROSAMUNDE	FRANCIE	LATIN
EPSTEIN	THERAPIST	POOL	LAUREN	CHEERLEADER

Izzy, Willy-Nilly

FRANCIE	DORA	LEG	TONY	JOEL
TREASURE	LINGARD	EPSTEIN	PIZZA	NICE
MARCO	HUMILIATED	FREE SPACE	POOL	MOTHER
SUZY	GRIGGERS	TREE	WEBBER	CRUTCHES
LITTLE	PENS	ROMEO	ADELIA	TRIVIAL

Izzy, Willy-Nilly

CHEERLEADER	THERAPIST	ROSAMUNDE	JACK	DEBORAH
DRUNK	BATIK	HAIRCUT	LEFT	LAUREN
SHOES	CLINGER	FREE SPACE	LATIN	BRAINS
LOOKS	JEALOUS	TRIVIAL	ADELIA	ROMEO
PENS	LITTLE	CRUTCHES	WEBBER	TREE

Izzy, Willy-Nilly

JACK	SUZY	LITTLE	PIZZA	LAUREN
MARCO	THERAPIST	CLINGER	LATIN	PENS
LOOKS	BATIK	FREE SPACE	EPSTEIN	CHEERLEADER
NICE	HUMILIATED	DORA	ROMEO	FRANCIE
JOEL	POOL	HAIRCUT	MOTHER	ROSAMUNDE

Izzy, Willy-Nilly

TONY	DRUNK	BEDROOM	DEBORAH	CRY
LEFT	LEG	JEALOUS	GRIGGERS	CRUTCHES
WEBBER	ADELIA	FREE SPACE	BRAINS	TRIVIAL
TREE	LINGARD	ROSAMUNDE	MOTHER	HAIRCUT
POOL	JOEL	FRANCIE	ROMEO	DORA

Izzy, Willy-Nilly

LATIN	ADELIA	TONY	LOOKS	CRY
JACK	PENS	CRUTCHES	JOEL	MOTHER
GRIGGERS	WEBBER	FREE SPACE	LEG	EPSTEIN
HUMILIATED	LINGARD	NICE	BATIK	DRUNK
PIZZA	TRIVIAL	FRANCIE	BRAINS	MARCO

Izzy, Willy-Nilly

TREASURE	POOL	LEFT	SUZY	ROSAMUNDE
LITTLE	SHOES	CHEERLEADER	THERAPIST	HAIRCUT
JEALOUS	CLINGER	FREE SPACE	BEDROOM	DEBORAH
LAUREN	DORA	MARCO	BRAINS	FRANCIE
TRIVIAL	PIZZA	DRUNK	BATIK	NICE

Izzy, Willy-Nilly

GRIGGERS	EPSTEIN	PENS	TREASURE	ROMEO
LITTLE	FRANCIE	LATIN	TONY	BRAINS
ROSAMUNDE	SHOES	FREE SPACE	JOEL	NICE
LEFT	HAIRCUT	LINGARD	DEBORAH	MOTHER
ADELIA	CRUTCHES	TREE	THERAPIST	POOL

Izzy, Willy-Nilly

LOOKS	LEG	DRUNK	JEALOUS	CRY
WEBBER	BEDROOM	LAUREN	MARCO	JACK
DORA	CLINGER	FREE SPACE	CHEERLEADER	PIZZA
HUMILIATED	BATIK	POOL	THERAPIST	TREE
CRUTCHES	ADELIA	MOTHER	DEBORAH	LINGARD

Izzy, Willy-Nilly

SHOES	EPSTEIN	CLINGER	PENS	LAUREN
DRUNK	NICE	ADELIA	MARCO	JOEL
HUMILIATED	JEALOUS	FREE SPACE	DEBORAH	TRIVIAL
GRIGGERS	BEDROOM	LEG	LOOKS	WEBBER
LATIN	LITTLE	SUZY	LEFT	JACK

Izzy, Willy-Nilly

TREE	TONY	FRANCIE	CRUTCHES	BRAINS
CRY	MOTHER	ROMEO	PIZZA	DORA
CHEERLEADER	HAIRCUT	FREE SPACE	LINGARD	ROSAMUNDE
THERAPIST	TREASURE	JACK	LEFT	SUZY
LITTLE	LATIN	WEBBER	LOOKS	LEG

Izzy, Willy-Nilly Vocabulary Word List

No.	Word	Clue/Definition
1.	AMPUTATED	Cut off through surgery
2.	ANEMIA	Having a reduced red blood count resulting in paleness & weakness
3.	ANGORA	Soft yarn used for sweaters
4.	ANTAGONIZE	Oppose; struggle against
5.	AVULSED	Tore away by surgical traction
6.	BANKRUPTCY	State of being unable to pay debts
7.	BATIK	Cloth decorated with dye--made by coating sections not to be dyed with removable wax
8.	BLAND	Tasteless
9.	BOASTING	Bragging
10.	BOISTEROUS	Noisy and lively
11.	CATHETER	Tube inserted into the body to drain urine from the bladder
12.	CERTIFIABLE	Insane
13.	CONDEMNED	Disapproved of strongly
14.	CONJUGATIONS	Inflectional forms of verbs
15.	CONTINGENCY	A possible, unforeseen, or accidental occurrence
16.	CONTUSIONS	Bruises
17.	CONVENIENT	Easy to do, use or get to; easily accessible
18.	DECREPIT	Worn out by old age
19.	DEFLATED	Made smaller or less important
20.	DIMINUTIVE	Very small
21.	DISJOINTED	Disconnected
22.	DIVERSIONARY	Serving to distract the attention
23.	DIVERT	Distract the attention of
24.	DOMESTIC	Having to do with the home or housekeeping
25.	DWINDLED	Diminished; made less
26.	EDIBLE	Anything fit to be eaten
27.	EMPHATICALLY	Done with emphasis or strength
28.	EVICT	Remove a tenant by legal procedures
29.	FIBULA	Long, thin outer bone of the human leg, between the knee and ankle
30.	GALE	Strong wind
31.	GENOISE	Rich, moist spongecake, often with a creamy filling between layers
32.	GLYCERIN	Odorless, colorless liquid used in skin lotion and other products
33.	GROUSED	Grumbled
34.	HUMILIATION	Feeling hurt pride or dignity being or seeming foolish
35.	IDEALIZE	Regard as perfect or more nearly perfect than is true
36.	ILLUSION	False perception of what one sees
37.	INADVERTENTLY	Unintentionally; without meaning to
38.	INCOMPETENT	Incapable; unskilled
39.	INCONVENIENT	Not favorable to one's comfort; difficult to do
40.	INDEFINITE	Not precise or clear in meaning; vague
41.	INDENTURED	____ servant: one who is (voluntarily or not) committed to working for someone for a number of years
42.	INTENSITY	Great energy of emotion, thought, or activity
43.	INTRUDING	Forcing oneself upon others without being asked
44.	IRRELEVANT	Not pertinent; not having anything to do with the matter at hand
45.	JUVENILE	Characteristic of children
46.	KOWTOW	Show respect by kneeling and touching the ground with the forehead

Izzy, Willy-Nilly Vocabulary Word List Continued

No. Word	Clue/Definition
47. LIBERATED	Set free; released
48. LINZERTORTE	Rich pastry made of almond dough & raspberry jam filling
49. LIVERY	Uniform worn by servants or those in some particular group or trade
50. MARINATING	Soaking meat or fish in a mixture of spices or liquids prior to cooking
51. NAUTILUS	Trademark for a kind of weight-lifting equipment
52. NECROSIS	Death of decay of tissue in a part of the body
53. NEEDLEPOINT	Embroidery of threads upon a canvas
54. NEGOTIATE	Bargain or discuss in order to reach an agreement
55. NOTORIOUS	Widely but unfavorably known
56. OBJECTIONS	Reasons for disapproving or disliking
57. OBJECTIVE	Without bias or prejudice
58. OBLIGE	Obligation of people of high social position to behave kindly toward others: noblesse ___
59. PEAKED	Thin and weak, as from illness
60. PEDIATRICIAN	Medical doctor specializing in the care of children
61. PEROSHKIS	Small pastry turnovers with a filling
62. PRECONCEPTIONS	Opinions formed in advance
63. PREJUDICES	Suspicion, intolerance, or irrational hatred of certain others
64. PRIVILEGED	Having a right, advantage, or favor that is withheld from certain or all others
65. PROSTHETIC	Artificial replacement part of the body
66. PSYCHOLOGICAL	Of the mind; mental
67. REASSURANCE	Restored confidence
68. RELUCTANCE	Unwillingness
69. REPERTOIRE	Special skills, techniques, etc. of a particular person
70. REPRESSING	Holding back
71. RUMMY	Card game
72. SARCASM	A taunting or cutting remark
73. SHALLOW	Lacking depth of character; superficial
74. SHEEN	Shininess; brightness; luster
75. SMOLDERING	Burning
76. SOLITAIRE	Card game played by one person
77. SOLITARY	Being alone
78. STABILIZED	Kept from changing
79. SUBTLETY	Ability to be delicately suggestive
80. THERAPY	Physical ___: treatment of injury by physical means rather than with drugs
81. TOUCHE	Word used to acknowledge a successful point
82. TRAUMA	Bodily injury, wound, or shock
83. UNDERESTIMATES	Sets too low of an estimate or judgement
84. VANITY	Excessively proud of oneself of one's qualities or possessions
85. WAILING	Long, pitiful crying
86. WOES	Great sorrows or troubles

Izzy, Willy-Nilly Vocabulary Fill In The Blanks 1

1. Sets too low of an estimate or judgement
2. Show respect by kneeling and touching the ground with the forehead
3. Artificial replacement part of the body
4. Made smaller or less important
5. Special skills, techniques, etc. of a particular person
6. Card game
7. Tore away by surgical traction
8. Rich pastry made of almond dough & raspberry jam filling
9. Holding back
10. Unintentionally; without meaning to
11. State of being unable to pay debts
12. Medical doctor specializing in the care of children
13. Restored confidence
14. Not precise or clear in meaning; vague
15. Lacking depth of character; superficial
16. Not favorable to one's comfort; difficult to do
17. Set free; released
18. Having to do with the home or housekeeping
19. Bragging
20. Uniform worn by servants or those in some particular group or trade

Izzy, Willy-Nilly Vocabulary Fill In The Blanks 1 Answer Key

UNDERESTIMATES	1. Sets too low of an estimate or judgement
KOWTOW	2. Show respect by kneeling and touching the ground with the forehead
PROSTHETIC	3. Artificial replacement part of the body
DEFLATED	4. Made smaller or less important
REPERTOIRE	5. Special skills, techniques, etc. of a particular person
RUMMY	6. Card game
AVULSED	7. Tore away by surgical traction
LINZERTORTE	8. Rich pastry made of almond dough & raspberry jam filling
REPRESSING	9. Holding back
INADVERTENTLY	10. Unintentionally; without meaning to
BANKRUPTCY	11. State of being unable to pay debts
PEDIATRICIAN	12. Medical doctor specializing in the care of children
REASSURANCE	13. Restored confidence
INDEFINITE	14. Not precise or clear in meaning; vague
SHALLOW	15. Lacking depth of character; superficial
INCONVENIENT	16. Not favorable to one's comfort; difficult to do
LIBERATED	17. Set free; released
DOMESTIC	18. Having to do with the home or housekeeping
BOASTING	19. Bragging
LIVERY	20. Uniform worn by servants or those in some particular group or trade

Izzy, Willy-Nilly Vocabulary Fill In The Blanks 2

_____ 1. Small pastry turnovers with a filling

_____ 2. Tasteless

_____ 3. Insane

_____ 4. A possible, unforeseen, or accidental occurrence

_____ 5. Burning

_____ 6. Tube inserted into the body to drain urine from the bladder

_____ 7. Suspicion, intolerance, or irrational hatred of certain others

_____ 8. Grumbled

_____ 9. A taunting or cutting remark

_____ 10. ____ servant: one who is (voluntarily or not) committed to working for someone for a number of years

_____ 11. Special skills, techniques, etc. of a particular person

_____ 12. Lacking depth of character; superficial

_____ 13. Forcing oneself upon others without being asked

_____ 14. Feeling hurt pride or dignity being or seeming foolish

_____ 15. Cut off through surgery

_____ 16. Odorless, colorless liquid used in skin lotion and other products

_____ 17. Show respect by kneeling and touching the ground with the forehead

_____ 18. Not pertinent; not having anything to do with the matter at hand

_____ 19. Uniform worn by servants or those in some particular group or trade

_____ 20. Cloth decorated with dye--made by coating sections not to be dyed with removable wax

Izzy, Willy-Nilly Vocabulary Fill In The Blanks 2 Answer Key

PEROSHKIS	1.	Small pastry turnovers with a filling
BLAND	2.	Tasteless
CERTIFIABLE	3.	Insane
CONTINGENCY	4.	A possible, unforeseen, or accidental occurrence
SMOLDERING	5.	Burning
CATHETER	6.	Tube inserted into the body to drain urine from the bladder
PREJUDICES	7.	Suspicion, intolerance, or irrational hatred of certain others
GROUSED	8.	Grumbled
SARCASM	9.	A taunting or cutting remark
INDENTURED	10.	____ servant: one who is (voluntarily or not) committed to working for someone for a number of years
REPERTOIRE	11.	Special skills, techniques, etc. of a particular person
SHALLOW	12.	Lacking depth of character; superficial
INTRUDING	13.	Forcing oneself upon others without being asked
HUMILIATION	14.	Feeling hurt pride or dignity being or seeming foolish
AMPUTATED	15.	Cut off through surgery
GLYCERIN	16.	Odorless, colorless liquid used in skin lotion and other products
KOWTOW	17.	Show respect by kneeling and touching the ground with the forehead
IRRELEVANT	18.	Not pertinent; not having anything to do with the matter at hand
LIVERY	19.	Uniform worn by servants or those in some particular group or trade
BATIK	20.	Cloth decorated with dye--made by coating sections not to be dyed with removable wax

Izzy, Willy-Nilly Vocabulary Fill In The Blanks 3

_____ 1. Tube inserted into the body to drain urine from the bladder
_____ 2. Tasteless
_____ 3. Of the mind; mental
_____ 4. Done with emphasis or strength
_____ 5. Embroidery of threads upon a canvas
_____ 6. Anything fit to be eaten
_____ 7. Opinions formed in advance
_____ 8. Rich pastry made of almond dough & raspberry jam filling
_____ 9. Death of decay of tissue in a part of the body
_____ 10. Noisy and lively
_____ 11. Great sorrows or troubles
_____ 12. Shininess; brightness; luster
_____ 13. Reasons for disapproving or disliking
_____ 14. Bruises
_____ 15. Ability to be delicately suggestive
_____ 16. Unintentionally; without meaning to
_____ 17. Artificial replacement part of the body
_____ 18. Serving to distract the attention
_____ 19. Being alone
_____ 20. State of being unable to pay debts

Izzy, Willy-Nilly Vocabulary Fill In The Blanks 3 Answer Key

CATHETER	1. Tube inserted into the body to drain urine from the bladder
BLAND	2. Tasteless
PSYCHOLOGICAL	3. Of the mind; mental
EMPHATICALLY	4. Done with emphasis or strength
NEEDLEPOINT	5. Embroidery of threads upon a canvas
EDIBLE	6. Anything fit to be eaten
PRECONCEPTIONS	7. Opinions formed in advance
LINZERTORTE	8. Rich pastry made of almond dough & raspberry jam filling
NECROSIS	9. Death of decay of tissue in a part of the body
BOISTEROUS	10. Noisy and lively
WOES	11. Great sorrows or troubles
SHEEN	12. Shininess; brightness; luster
OBJECTIONS	13. Reasons for disapproving or disliking
CONTUSIONS	14. Bruises
SUBTLETY	15. Ability to be delicately suggestive
INADVERTENTLY	16. Unintentionally; without meaning to
PROSTHETIC	17. Artificial replacement part of the body
DIVERSIONARY	18. Serving to distract the attention
SOLITARY	19. Being alone
BANKRUPTCY	20. State of being unable to pay debts

Izzy, Willy-Nilly Vocabulary Fill In The Blanks 4

1. Soft yarn used for sweaters
2. Having to do with the home or housekeeping
3. Rich pastry made of almond dough & raspberry jam filling
4. Card game played by one person
5. Set free; released
6. Word used to acknowledge a successful point
7. Reasons for disapproving or disliking
8. Physical ___: treatment of injury by physical means rather than with drugs
9. Remove a tenant by legal procedures
10. Disapproved of strongly
11. Soaking meat or fish in a mixture of spices or liquids prior to cooking
12. False perception of what one sees
13. Having a right, advantage, or favor that is withheld from certain or all others
14. Characteristic of children
15. Kept from changing
16. Small pastry turnovers with a filling
17. Forcing oneself upon others without being asked
18. Unwillingness
19. Of the mind; mental
20. Ability to be delicately suggestive

Izzy, Willy-Nilly Vocabulary Fill In The Blanks 4 Answer Key

ANGORA	1. Soft yarn used for sweaters
DOMESTIC	2. Having to do with the home or housekeeping
LINZERTORTE	3. Rich pastry made of almond dough & raspberry jam filling
SOLITAIRE	4. Card game played by one person
LIBERATED	5. Set free; released
TOUCHE	6. Word used to acknowledge a successful point
OBJECTIONS	7. Reasons for disapproving or disliking
THERAPY	8. Physical ___: treatment of injury by physical means rather than with drugs
EVICT	9. Remove a tenant by legal procedures
CONDEMNED	10. Disapproved of strongly
MARINATING	11. Soaking meat or fish in a mixture of spices or liquids prior to cooking
ILLUSION	12. False perception of what one sees
PRIVILEGED	13. Having a right, advantage, or favor that is withheld from certain or all others
JUVENILE	14. Characteristic of children
STABILIZED	15. Kept from changing
PEROSHKIS	16. Small pastry turnovers with a filling
INTRUDING	17. Forcing oneself upon others without being asked
RELUCTANCE	18. Unwillingness
PSYCHOLOGICAL	19. Of the mind; mental
SUBTLETY	20. Ability to be delicately suggestive

Izzy, Willy-Nilly Vocabulary Matching 1

___ 1. DECREPIT
___ 2. PREJUDICES
___ 3. GLYCERIN
___ 4. WAILING
___ 5. NEEDLEPOINT
___ 6. INADVERTENTLY
___ 7. DIVERSIONARY
___ 8. AVULSED
___ 9. NOTORIOUS
___ 10. AMPUTATED
___ 11. INDENTURED
___ 12. NECROSIS
___ 13. BLAND
___ 14. PEAKED
___ 15. EDIBLE
___ 16. THERAPY
___ 17. OBLIGE
___ 18. WOES
___ 19. OBJECTIONS
___ 20. CONTINGENCY
___ 21. KOWTOW
___ 22. ANEMIA
___ 23. PROSTHETIC
___ 24. PEDIATRICIAN
___ 25. TRAUMA

A. Physical ___: treatment of injury by physical means rather than with drugs
B. Widely but unfavorably known
C. Worn out by old age
D. Reasons for disapproving or disliking
E. Thin and weak, as from illness
F. Having a reduced red blood count resulting in paleness & weakness
G. Great sorrows or troubles
H. Bodily injury, wound, or shock
I. Unintentionally; without meaning to
J. Death of decay of tissue in a part of the body
K. Embroidery of threads upon a canvas
L. Tore away by surgical traction
M. Odorless, colorless liquid used in skin lotion and other products
N. Artificial replacement part of the body
O. Cut off through surgery
P. Tasteless
Q. ____ servant: one who is (voluntarily or not) committed to working for someone for a number of years
R. Show respect by kneeling and touching the ground with the forehead
S. Long, pitiful crying
T. Medical doctor specializing in the care of children
U. Obligation of people of high social position to behave kindly toward others: noblesse ___
V. Anything fit to be eaten
W. Suspicion, intolerance, or irrational hatred of certain others
X. A possible, unforeseen, or accidental occurrence
Y. Serving to distract the attention

Izzy, Willy-Nilly Vocabulary Matching 1 Answer Key

C - 1.	DECREPIT	A.	Physical ___: treatment of injury by physical means rather than with drugs
W - 2.	PREJUDICES	B.	Widely but unfavorably known
M - 3.	GLYCERIN	C.	Worn out by old age
S - 4.	WAILING	D.	Reasons for disapproving or disliking
K - 5.	NEEDLEPOINT	E.	Thin and weak, as from illness
I - 6.	INADVERTENTLY	F.	Having a reduced red blood count resulting in paleness & weakness
Y - 7.	DIVERSIONARY	G.	Great sorrows or troubles
L - 8.	AVULSED	H.	Bodily injury, wound, or shock
B - 9.	NOTORIOUS	I.	Unintentionally; without meaning to
O -10.	AMPUTATED	J.	Death of decay of tissue in a part of the body
Q -11.	INDENTURED	K.	Embroidery of threads upon a canvas
J -12.	NECROSIS	L.	Tore away by surgical traction
P -13.	BLAND	M.	Odorless, colorless liquid used in skin lotion and other products
E -14.	PEAKED	N.	Artificial replacement part of the body
V -15.	EDIBLE	O.	Cut off through surgery
A -16.	THERAPY	P.	Tasteless
U -17.	OBLIGE	Q.	____ servant: one who is (voluntarily or not) committed to working for someone for a number of years
G -18.	WOES	R.	Show respect by kneeling and touching the ground with the forehead
D -19.	OBJECTIONS	S.	Long, pitiful crying
X -20.	CONTINGENCY	T.	Medical doctor specializing in the care of children
R -21.	KOWTOW	U.	Obligation of people of high social position to behave kindly toward others: noblesse ___
F -22.	ANEMIA	V.	Anything fit to be eaten
N -23.	PROSTHETIC	W.	Suspicion, intolerance, or irrational hatred of certain others
T -24.	PEDIATRICIAN	X.	A possible, unforeseen, or accidental occurrence
H -25.	TRAUMA	Y.	Serving to distract the attention

Izzy, Willy-Nilly Vocabulary Matching 2

___ 1. EDIBLE
___ 2. PEAKED
___ 3. UNDERESTIMATES
___ 4. REPRESSING
___ 5. IDEALIZE
___ 6. RELUCTANCE
___ 7. CATHETER
___ 8. SMOLDERING
___ 9. NEGOTIATE
___10. BOASTING
___11. CONDEMNED
___12. MARINATING
___13. PSYCHOLOGICAL
___14. INTENSITY
___15. ANTAGONIZE
___16. PREJUDICES
___17. DECREPIT
___18. INTRUDING
___19. BLAND
___20. GENOISE
___21. REASSURANCE
___22. NEEDLEPOINT
___23. INCOMPETENT
___24. INCONVENIENT
___25. PEROSHKIS

A. Incapable; unskilled
B. Anything fit to be eaten
C. Disapproved of strongly
D. Worn out by old age
E. Bragging
F. Not favorable to one's comfort; difficult to do
G. Thin and weak, as from illness
H. Regard as perfect or more nearly perfect than is true
I. Tasteless
J. Holding back
K. Rich, moist spongecake, often with a creamy filling between layers
L. Tube inserted into the body to drain urine from the bladder
M. Soaking meat or fish in a mixture of spices or liquids prior to cooking
N. Oppose; struggle against
O. Forcing oneself upon others without being asked
P. Restored confidence
Q. Great energy of emotion, thought, or activity
R. Bargain or discuss in order to reach an agreement
S. Of the mind; mental
T. Suspicion, intolerance, or irrational hatred of certain others
U. Embroidery of threads upon a canvas
V. Small pastry turnovers with a filling
W. Sets too low of an estimate or judgement
X. Burning
Y. Unwillingness

Izzy, Willy-Nilly Vocabulary Matching 2 Answer Key

B - 1. EDIBLE
G - 2. PEAKED
W - 3. UNDERESTIMATES
J - 4. REPRESSING
H - 5. IDEALIZE
Y - 6. RELUCTANCE
L - 7. CATHETER
X - 8. SMOLDERING
R - 9. NEGOTIATE
E - 10. BOASTING
C - 11. CONDEMNED
M - 12. MARINATING
S - 13. PSYCHOLOGICAL
Q - 14. INTENSITY
N - 15. ANTAGONIZE
T - 16. PREJUDICES
D - 17. DECREPIT
O - 18. INTRUDING
I - 19. BLAND
K - 20. GENOISE
P - 21. REASSURANCE
U - 22. NEEDLEPOINT
A - 23. INCOMPETENT
F - 24. INCONVENIENT
V - 25. PEROSHKIS

A. Incapable; unskilled
B. Anything fit to be eaten
C. Disapproved of strongly
D. Worn out by old age
E. Bragging
F. Not favorable to one's comfort; difficult to do
G. Thin and weak, as from illness
H. Regard as perfect or more nearly perfect than is true
I. Tasteless
J. Holding back
K. Rich, moist spongecake, often with a creamy filling between layers
L. Tube inserted into the body to drain urine from the bladder
M. Soaking meat or fish in a mixture of spices or liquids prior to cooking
N. Oppose; struggle against
O. Forcing oneself upon others without being asked
P. Restored confidence
Q. Great energy of emotion, thought, or activity
R. Bargain or discuss in order to reach an agreement
S. Of the mind; mental
T. Suspicion, intolerance, or irrational hatred of certain others
U. Embroidery of threads upon a canvas
V. Small pastry turnovers with a filling
W. Sets too low of an estimate or judgement
X. Burning
Y. Unwillingness

Izzy, Willy-Nilly Vocabulary Matching 3

___ 1. INADVERTENTLY   A. Serving to distract the attention
___ 2. VANITY   B. Burning
___ 3. INDEFINITE   C. Opinions formed in advance
___ 4. INTRUDING   D. Bodily injury, wound, or shock
___ 5. CONTUSIONS   E. Inflectional forms of verbs
___ 6. PEAKED   F. Forcing oneself upon others without being asked
___ 7. TOUCHE   G. Bruises
___ 8. CONJUGATIONS   H. Not favorable to one's comfort; difficult to do
___ 9. DWINDLED   I. Oppose; struggle against
___ 10. SUBTLETY   J. Kept from changing
___ 11. EDIBLE   K. Diminished; made less
___ 12. PROSTHETIC   L. Anything fit to be eaten
___ 13. TRAUMA   M. Ability to be delicately suggestive
___ 14. SMOLDERING   N. Thin and weak, as from illness
___ 15. STABILIZED   O. ____ servant: one who is (voluntarily or not) committed to working for someone for a number of years
___ 16. INCONVENIENT   P. Not precise or clear in meaning; vague
___ 17. PRECONCEPTIONS   Q. Unintentionally; without meaning to
___ 18. DIMINUTIVE   R. Artificial replacement part of the body
___ 19. ANTAGONIZE   S. Excessively proud of oneself of one's qualities or possessions
___ 20. DIVERSIONARY   T. Set free; released
___ 21. LIBERATED   U. Medical doctor specializing in the care of children
___ 22. PEDIATRICIAN   V. Word used to acknowledge a successful point
___ 23. NEEDLEPOINT   W. Reasons for disapproving or disliking
___ 24. OBJECTIONS   X. Very small
___ 25. INDENTURED   Y. Embroidery of threads upon a canvas

Izzy, Willy-Nilly Vocabulary Matching 3 Answer Key

Q - 1. INADVERTENTLY — A. Serving to distract the attention
S - 2. VANITY — B. Burning
P - 3. INDEFINITE — C. Opinions formed in advance
F - 4. INTRUDING — D. Bodily injury, wound, or shock
G - 5. CONTUSIONS — E. Inflectional forms of verbs
N - 6. PEAKED — F. Forcing oneself upon others without being asked
V - 7. TOUCHE — G. Bruises
E - 8. CONJUGATIONS — H. Not favorable to one's comfort; difficult to do
K - 9. DWINDLED — I. Oppose; struggle against
M - 10. SUBTLETY — J. Kept from changing
L - 11. EDIBLE — K. Diminished; made less
R - 12. PROSTHETIC — L. Anything fit to be eaten
D - 13. TRAUMA — M. Ability to be delicately suggestive
B - 14. SMOLDERING — N. Thin and weak, as from illness
J - 15. STABILIZED — O. ____ servant: one who is (voluntarily or not) committed to working for someone for a number of years
H - 16. INCONVENIENT — P. Not precise or clear in meaning; vague
C - 17. PRECONCEPTIONS — Q. Unintentionally; without meaning to
X - 18. DIMINUTIVE — R. Artificial replacement part of the body
I - 19. ANTAGONIZE — S. Excessively proud of oneself of one's qualities or possessions
A - 20. DIVERSIONARY — T. Set free; released
T - 21. LIBERATED — U. Medical doctor specializing in the care of children
U - 22. PEDIATRICIAN — V. Word used to acknowledge a successful point
Y - 23. NEEDLEPOINT — W. Reasons for disapproving or disliking
W - 24. OBJECTIONS — X. Very small
O - 25. INDENTURED — Y. Embroidery of threads upon a canvas

Izzy, Willy-Nilly Vocabulary Matching 4

___ 1. GALE
___ 2. SHEEN
___ 3. PSYCHOLOGICAL
___ 4. WOES
___ 5. PEAKED
___ 6. MARINATING
___ 7. BOISTEROUS
___ 8. SOLITARY
___ 9. RUMMY
___10. REASSURANCE
___11. REPERTOIRE
___12. CONJUGATIONS
___13. DIVERSIONARY
___14. IDEALIZE
___15. DEFLATED
___16. PEDIATRICIAN
___17. IRRELEVANT
___18. CERTIFIABLE
___19. INADVERTENTLY
___20. PRECONCEPTIONS
___21. EDIBLE
___22. AVULSED
___23. LIBERATED
___24. ANEMIA
___25. TRAUMA

A. Inflectional forms of verbs
B. Great sorrows or troubles
C. Having a reduced red blood count resulting in paleness & weakness
D. Regard as perfect or more nearly perfect than is true
E. Serving to distract the attention
F. Tore away by surgical traction
G. Strong wind
H. Of the mind; mental
I. Shininess; brightness; luster
J. Opinions formed in advance
K. Being alone
L. Card game
M. Unintentionally; without meaning to
N. Medical doctor specializing in the care of children
O. Made smaller or less important
P. Special skills, techniques, etc. of a particular person
Q. Soaking meat or fish in a mixture of spices or liquids prior to cooking
R. Thin and weak, as from illness
S. Insane
T. Anything fit to be eaten
U. Noisy and lively
V. Set free; released
W. Restored confidence
X. Not pertinent; not having anything to do with the matter at hand
Y. Bodily injury, wound, or shock

Izzy, Willy-Nilly Vocabulary Matching 4 Answer Key

G - 1. GALE
I - 2. SHEEN
H - 3. PSYCHOLOGICAL
B - 4. WOES
R - 5. PEAKED
Q - 6. MARINATING
U - 7. BOISTEROUS
K - 8. SOLITARY
L - 9. RUMMY
W - 10. REASSURANCE
P - 11. REPERTOIRE
A - 12. CONJUGATIONS
E - 13. DIVERSIONARY
D - 14. IDEALIZE
O - 15. DEFLATED
N - 16. PEDIATRICIAN
X - 17. IRRELEVANT
S - 18. CERTIFIABLE
M - 19. INADVERTENTLY
J - 20. PRECONCEPTIONS
T - 21. EDIBLE
F - 22. AVULSED
V - 23. LIBERATED
C - 24. ANEMIA
Y - 25. TRAUMA

A. Inflectional forms of verbs
B. Great sorrows or troubles
C. Having a reduced red blood count resulting in paleness & weakness
D. Regard as perfect or more nearly perfect than is true
E. Serving to distract the attention
F. Tore away by surgical traction
G. Strong wind
H. Of the mind; mental
I. Shininess; brightness; luster
J. Opinions formed in advance
K. Being alone
L. Card game
M. Unintentionally; without meaning to
N. Medical doctor specializing in the care of children
O. Made smaller or less important
P. Special skills, techniques, etc. of a particular person
Q. Soaking meat or fish in a mixture of spices or liquids prior to cooking
R. Thin and weak, as from illness
S. Insane
T. Anything fit to be eaten
U. Noisy and lively
V. Set free; released
W. Restored confidence
X. Not pertinent; not having anything to do with the matter at hand
Y. Bodily injury, wound, or shock

Izzy, Willy-Nilly Vocabulary Magic Squares 1

Match the definition with the vocabulary word. Put your answers in the magic squares below. When your answers are correct, all columns and rows will add to the same number.

A. ANTAGONIZE
B. IRRELEVANT
C. SUBTLETY
D. RUMMY
E. NEGOTIATE
F. RELUCTANCE
G. DISJOINTED
H. THERAPY
I. PEROSHKIS
J. VANITY
K. PEDIATRICIAN
L. PRECONCEPTIONS
M. NECROSIS
N. IDEALIZE
O. BOISTEROUS
P. TRAUMA

1. Noisy and lively
2. Card game
3. Excessively proud of oneself of one's qualities or possessions
4. Bargain or discuss in order to reach an agreement
5. Small pastry turnovers with a filling
6. Unwillingness
7. Bodily injury, wound, or shock
8. Ability to be delicately suggestive
9. Physical ___: treatment of injury by physical means rather than with drugs
10. Medical doctor specializing in the care of children
11. Oppose; struggle against
12. Regard as perfect or more nearly perfect than is true
13. Not pertinent; not having anything to do with the matter at hand
14. Death of decay of tissue in a part of the body
15. Disconnected
16. Opinions formed in advance

A=	B=	C=	D=
E=	F=	G=	H=
I=	J=	K=	L=
M=	N=	O=	P=

Izzy, Willy-Nilly Vocabulary Magic Squares 1 Answer Key

Match the definition with the vocabulary word. Put your answers in the magic squares below. When your answers are correct, all columns and rows will add to the same number.

A. ANTAGONIZE
B. IRRELEVANT
C. SUBTLETY
D. RUMMY
E. NEGOTIATE
F. RELUCTANCE
G. DISJOINTED
H. THERAPY
I. PEROSHKIS
J. VANITY
K. PEDIATRICIAN
L. PRECONCEPTIONS
M. NECROSIS
N. IDEALIZE
O. BOISTEROUS
P. TRAUMA

1. Noisy and lively
2. Card game
3. Excessively proud of oneself of one's qualities or possessions
4. Bargain or discuss in order to reach an agreement
5. Small pastry turnovers with a filling
6. Unwillingness
7. Bodily injury, wound, or shock
8. Ability to be delicately suggestive
9. Physical ___: treatment of injury by physical means rather than with drugs
10. Medical doctor specializing in the care of children
11. Oppose; struggle against
12. Regard as perfect or more nearly perfect than is true
13. Not pertinent; not having anything to do with the matter at hand
14. Death of decay of tissue in a part of the body
15. Disconnected
16. Opinions formed in advance

A=11	B=13	C=8	D=2
E=4	F=6	G=15	H=9
I=5	J=3	K=10	L=16
M=14	N=12	O=1	P=7

Izzy, Willy-Nilly Vocabulary Magic Squares 2

Match the definition with the vocabulary word. Put your answers in the magic squares below. When your answers are correct, all columns and rows will add to the same number.

A. SARCASM
B. PEDIATRICIAN
C. PROSTHETIC
D. ANTAGONIZE
E. GENOISE
F. REASSURANCE
G. SOLITAIRE
H. STABILIZED
I. CONTUSIONS
J. DWINDLED
K. PSYCHOLOGICAL
L. SHEEN
M. DECREPIT
N. TRAUMA
O. AMPUTATED
P. OBLIGE

1. Cut off through surgery
2. Diminished; made less
3. Kept from changing
4. A taunting or cutting remark
5. Oppose; struggle against
6. Rich, moist spongecake, often with a creamy filling between layers
7. Of the mind; mental
8. Bodily injury, wound, or shock
9. Restored confidence
10. Artificial replacement part of the body
11. Worn out by old age
12. Shininess; brightness; luster
13. Bruises
14. Obligation of people of high social position to behave kindly toward others: noblesse ___
15. Medical doctor specializing in the care of children
16. Card game played by one person

A=	B=	C=	D=
E=	F=	G=	H=
I=	J=	K=	L=
M=	N=	O=	P=

Izzy, Willy-Nilly Vocabulary Magic Squares 2 Answer Key

Match the definition with the vocabulary word. Put your answers in the magic squares below. When your answers are correct, all columns and rows will add to the same number.

A. SARCASM
B. PEDIATRICIAN
C. PROSTHETIC
D. ANTAGONIZE
E. GENOISE
F. REASSURANCE
G. SOLITAIRE
H. STABILIZED
I. CONTUSIONS
J. DWINDLED
K. PSYCHOLOGICAL
L. SHEEN
M. DECREPIT
N. TRAUMA
O. AMPUTATED
P. OBLIGE

1. Cut off through surgery
2. Diminished; made less
3. Kept from changing
4. A taunting or cutting remark
5. Oppose; struggle against
6. Rich, moist spongecake, often with a creamy filling between layers
7. Of the mind; mental
8. Bodily injury, wound, or shock
9. Restored confidence
10. Artificial replacement part of the body
11. Worn out by old age
12. Shininess; brightness; luster
13. Bruises
14. Obligation of people of high social position to behave kindly toward others: noblesse ___
15. Medical doctor specializing in the care of children
16. Card game played by one person

A=4	B=15	C=10	D=5
E=6	F=9	G=16	H=3
I=13	J=2	K=7	L=12
M=11	N=8	O=1	P=14

Izzy, Willy-Nilly Vocabulary Magic Squares 3

Match the definition with the vocabulary word. Put your answers in the magic squares below. When your answers are correct, all columns and rows will add to the same number.

A. LIBERATED
B. SARCASM
C. KOWTOW
D. INTRUDING
E. DIMINUTIVE
F. LIVERY
G. MARINATING
H. LINZERTORTE
I. OBLIGE
J. INCOMPETENT
K. INTENSITY
L. CONVENIENT
M. DISJOINTED
N. REPRESSING
O. INDEFINITE
P. REASSURANCE

1. A taunting or cutting remark
2. Soaking meat or fish in a mixture of spices or liquids prior to cooking
3. Great energy of emotion, thought, or activity
4. Holding back
5. Disconnected
6. Easy to do, use or get to; easily accessible
7. Rich pastry made of almond dough & raspberry jam filling
8. Set free; released
9. Restored confidence
10. Obligation of people of high social position to behave kindly toward others: noblesse ___
11. Very small
12. Forcing oneself upon others without being asked
13. Show respect by kneeling and touching the ground with the forehead
14. Uniform worn by servants or those in some particular group or trade
15. Incapable; unskilled
16. Not precise or clear in meaning; vague

A=	B=	C=	D=
E=	F=	G=	H=
I=	J=	K=	L=
M=	N=	O=	P=

Izzy, Willy-Nilly Vocabulary Magic Squares 3 Answer Key

Match the definition with the vocabulary word. Put your answers in the magic squares below. When your answers are correct, all columns and rows will add to the same number.

A. LIBERATED
B. SARCASM
C. KOWTOW
D. INTRUDING
E. DIMINUTIVE
F. LIVERY
G. MARINATING
H. LINZERTORTE
I. OBLIGE
J. INCOMPETENT
K. INTENSITY
L. CONVENIENT
M. DISJOINTED
N. REPRESSING
O. INDEFINITE
P. REASSURANCE

1. A taunting or cutting remark
2. Soaking meat or fish in a mixture of spices or liquids prior to cooking
3. Great energy of emotion, thought, or activity
4. Holding back
5. Disconnected
6. Easy to do, use or get to; easily accessible
7. Rich pastry made of almond dough & raspberry jam filling
8. Set free; released
9. Restored confidence
10. Obligation of people of high social position to behave kindly toward others: noblesse ___
11. Very small
12. Forcing oneself upon others without being asked
13. Show respect by kneeling and touching the ground with the forehead
14. Uniform worn by servants or those in some particular group or trade
15. Incapable; unskilled
16. Not precise or clear in meaning; vague

A=8	B=1	C=13	D=12
E=11	F=14	G=2	H=7
I=10	J=15	K=3	L=6
M=5	N=4	O=16	P=9

Izzy, Willy-Nilly Vocabulary Magic Squares 4

Match the definition with the vocabulary word. Put your answers in the magic squares below. When your answers are correct, all columns and rows will add to the same number.

A. INCOMPETENT
B. NAUTILUS
C. DIVERSIONARY
D. INDENTURED
E. ANEMIA
F. CERTIFIABLE
G. PREJUDICES
H. LIBERATED
I. REPRESSING
J. SARCASM
K. AMPUTATED
L. STABILIZED
M. PRECONCEPTIONS
N. HUMILIATION
O. SHALLOW
P. DWINDLED

1. Serving to distract the attention
2. A taunting or cutting remark
3. Insane
4. Lacking depth of character; superficial
5. Diminished; made less
6. Having a reduced red blood count resulting in paleness & weakness
7. Holding back
8. ____ servant: one who is (voluntarily or not) committed to working for someone for a number of years
9. Opinions formed in advance
10. Set free; released
11. Kept from changing
12. Incapable; unskilled
13. Trademark for a kind of weight-lifting equipment
14. Cut off through surgery
15. Suspicion, intolerance, or irrational hatred of certain others
16. Feeling hurt pride or dignity being or seeming foolish

A=	B=	C=	D=
E=	F=	G=	H=
I=	J=	K=	L=
M=	N=	O=	P=

Izzy, Willy-Nilly Vocabulary Magic Squares 4 Answer Key

Match the definition with the vocabulary word. Put your answers in the magic squares below. When your answers are correct, all columns and rows will add to the same number.

A. INCOMPETENT
B. NAUTILUS
C. DIVERSIONARY
D. INDENTURED
E. ANEMIA
F. CERTIFIABLE
G. PREJUDICES
H. LIBERATED
I. REPRESSING
J. SARCASM
K. AMPUTATED
L. STABILIZED
M. PRECONCEPTIONS
N. HUMILIATION
O. SHALLOW
P. DWINDLED

1. Serving to distract the attention
2. A taunting or cutting remark
3. Insane
4. Lacking depth of character; superficial
5. Diminished; made less
6. Having a reduced red blood count resulting in paleness & weakness
7. Holding back
8. ____ servant: one who is (voluntarily or not) committed to working for someone for a number of years
9. Opinions formed in advance
10. Set free; released
11. Kept from changing
12. Incapable; unskilled
13. Trademark for a kind of weight-lifting equipment
14. Cut off through surgery
15. Suspicion, intolerance, or irrational hatred of certain others
16. Feeling hurt pride or dignity being or seeming foolish

A=12	B=13	C=1	D=8
E=6	F=3	G=15	H=10
I=7	J=2	K=14	L=11
M=9	N=16	O=4	P=5

Izzy, Willy-Nilly Vocabulary Word Search 1

A	N	G	O	R	A	I	N	D	E	N	T	U	R	E	D	O	Q
N	V	P	R	I	V	I	L	E	G	E	D	C	L	E	O	B	B
T	A	S	R	U	M	M	Y	S	Q	T	Y	A	S	B	D	J	N
A	N	A	G	C	J	S	B	L	O	L	G	U	L	E	K	E	C
G	I	R	N	O	F	I	B	U	L	A	O	I	L	Y	M	C	P
O	T	C	I	N	S	B	C	V	D	R	G	D	P	P	W	T	S
N	Y	A	S	T	X	H	M	A	G	E	N	A	H	E	V	I	Y
I	N	S	S	U	E	X	Y	S	C	I	R	A	X	D	B	V	C
Z	P	M	E	S	R	Q	R	N	W	E	T	N	L	I	O	E	H
E	W	P	R	I	M	R	A	D	H	I	W	E	Y	B	A	R	O
M	S	O	P	O	D	R	T	T	C	L	O	M	F	L	S	G	L
W	U	P	E	N	U	G	I	A	G	X	T	I	D	E	T	K	O
R	B	G	R	S	W	B	L	A	N	D	W	A	I	L	I	N	G
P	T	L	S	Z	M	L	O	Y	P	I	O	D	G	T	N	E	I
Z	L	A	P	N	Y	W	S	W	C	V	K	S	A	Z	G	C	C
D	E	N	M	E	D	N	O	C	T	E	B	B	N	H	E	R	A
R	T	R	A	U	M	A	T	L	G	R	E	R	F	V	O	L	L
P	Y	Q	N	E	G	O	T	I	A	T	E	I	M	W	I	S	P
I	D	E	A	L	I	Z	E	P	T	H	F	T	N	N	C	I	D
D	E	F	L	A	T	E	D	E	S	I	O	N	E	G	T	S	F

A taunting or cutting remark (7)
Ability to be delicately suggestive (8)
Anything fit to be eaten (6)
Bargain or discuss in order to reach an agreement (9)
Being alone (8)
Bodily injury, wound, or shock (6)
Bragging (8)
Bruises (10)
Card game (5)
Cloth decorated with dye--made by coating sections not to be dyed with removable wax (5)
Death of decay of tissue in a part of the body (8)
Diminished; made less (8)
Disapproved of strongly (9)
Distract the attention of (6)
Done with emphasis or strength (12)
Excessively proud of oneself of one's qualities or possessions (6)
Great sorrows or troubles (4)
Grumbled (7)
Having a reduced red blood count resulting in paleness & weakness (6)
Having a right, advantage, or favor that is withheld from certain or all others (10)
Holding back (10)
Long, pitiful crying (7)
Long, thin outer bone of the human leg, between the knee and ankle (6)
Made smaller or less important (8)
Obligation of people of high social position to behave kindly toward others: noblesse ___ (6)
Odorless, colorless liquid used in skin lotion and other products (8)
Of the mind; mental (13)
Oppose; struggle against (10)
Physical ___: treatment of injury by physical means rather than with drugs (7)
Regard as perfect or more nearly perfect than is true (8)
Remove a tenant by legal procedures (5)
Restored confidence (11)
Rich, moist spongecake, often with a creamy filling between layers (7)
Shininess; brightness; luster (5)
Show respect by kneeling and touching the ground with the forehead (6)
Soft yarn used for sweaters (6)
Strong wind (4)
Tasteless (5)
Tore away by surgical traction (7)
Without bias or prejudice (9)
Word used to acknowledge a successful point (6)
____ servant: one who is (voluntarily or not) committed to working for someone for a number of years

Izzy, Willy-Nilly Vocabulary Word Search 1 Answer Key

```
A  N  G  O  R  A  I  N  D  E  N  T  U  R  E  D  O
N  V  P  R  I  V  I  L  E  G  E  D     L  E  O  B
T  A  S  R  U  M  M  Y  S        T     A  S  B  D  J
A  N  A  G  C              L     O     G  U  L  E  E
G  I  R  N  O  F  I  B  U  L  A  O  I  L  Y  M  C  P
O  T  C  I  N        C  V     R  G  D  P  P     T  S
N  Y  A  S  T        H     A  G  E  N  A  H  E  I  Y
I     S  S  U  E           Y     C  I  R  A  D  B  V  C
Z     M  E  S              R     N  W  E  T  N  O  E  H
E  W     R  I              A  T  D  H  I  W  E  A  S  O
   S  O  P  O     R  T     T  C     O  M     L  S     L
   U     E  N  U  G  I  A        T  I        E  T  K  O
   B     R  S     B  L  A  N  D  W  A        L  I  N  G
   T     S        L  O  Y        I  O        T  N  E  I
   L  A        Y        S     C  V  K     A     G  C  C
D  E  N  M  E  D  N  O  C        E        B  N  E  R  A
R  T  R  A  U  M  A              R  R     E     V  O  L
   Y     N  E  G  O  T  I  A  T  E     I     I  S
I  D  E  A  L  I  Z  E           H        N     C  I
D  E  F  L  A  T  E  D  E  S     I  O  N  E  G  T  S
```

A taunting or cutting remark (7)
Ability to be delicately suggestive (8)
Anything fit to be eaten (6)
Bargain or discuss in order to reach an agreement (9)
Being alone (8)
Bodily injury, wound, or shock (6)
Bragging (8)
Bruises (10)
Card game (5)
Cloth decorated with dye--made by coating sections not to be dyed with removable wax (5)
Death of decay of tissue in a part of the body (8)
Diminished; made less (8)
Disapproved of strongly (9)
Distract the attention of (6)
Done with emphasis or strength (12)
Excessively proud of oneself of one's qualities or possessions (6)
Great sorrows or troubles (4)
Grumbled (7)
Having a reduced red blood count resulting in paleness & weakness (6)
Having a right, advantage, or favor that is withheld from certain or all others (10)
Holding back (10)
Long, pitiful crying (7)
Long, thin outer bone of the human leg, between the knee and ankle (6)
Made smaller or less important (8)
Obligation of people of high social position to behave kindly toward others: noblesse ___ (6)
Odorless, colorless liquid used in skin lotion and other products (8)
Of the mind; mental (13)
Oppose; struggle against (10)
Physical ___: treatment of injury by physical means rather than with drugs (7)
Regard as perfect or more nearly perfect than is true (8)
Remove a tenant by legal procedures (5)
Restored confidence (11)
Rich, moist spongecake, often with a creamy filling between layers (7)
Shininess; brightness; luster (5)
Show respect by kneeling and touching the ground with the forehead (6)
Soft yarn used for sweaters (6)
Strong wind (4)
Tasteless (5)
Tore away by surgical traction (7)
Without bias or prejudice (9)
Word used to acknowledge a successful point (6)
____ servant: one who is (voluntarily or not) committed to working for someone for a number of years

Izzy, Willy-Nilly Vocabulary Word Search 2

```
J U V E N I L E N G M E T E F R P S
N A L U B I F I L R L R H I Q U S B
Y O R Y V V R V L B A C B N W M Y F
N G T E X E L Z A U U Q H T X M C C
A N R O C L B I M O R Z J R G Y H Y
U Y V Y R B F A T E S P Q U S A O H
T R L Q F I C I T S E M O D T O L Q
I G L W T D O E W I R P E I A B O E
L P R R E E H U H E K T Z N B L G T
U Q E K K T D S S V N J I G I I I N
S C A B A O H W A I L I N G L G C L
C E S C O E B E O C D S O X I E A K
P B S S E I Z J R T H E G R Z R L Q
S Y U N Y N S M E A K B A N E M I A
M T R E V I D T L C P A T L D Z X C
Q I A Q D V Q L E M T Y N B I Z P Y
Z N N P P C O H W R R I A G L Z D C
Y A C K O W T O W M O M O T O A E Z
F V E T I P E R C E D U X N V R N X
G E N O I S E S A R C A S M S T A D
```

A taunting or cutting remark (7)
Anything fit to be eaten (6)
Bodily injury, wound, or shock (6)
Card game (5)
Characteristic of children (8)
Cloth decorated with dye--made by coating sections not to be dyed with removable wax (5)
Disconnected (10)
Distract the attention of (6)
Excessively proud of oneself of one's qualities or possessions (6)
Forcing oneself upon others without being asked (9)
Great sorrows or troubles (4)
Having a reduced red blood count resulting in paleness & weakness (6)
Having to do with the home or housekeeping (8)
Insane (11)
Kept from changing (10)
Lacking depth of character; superficial (7)
Long, pitiful crying (7)
Long, thin outer bone of the human leg, between the knee and ankle (6)
Noisy and lively (10)
Obligation of people of high social position to behave kindly toward others: noblesse ___ (6)
Odorless, colorless liquid used in skin lotion and other products (8)

Of the mind; mental (13)
Oppose; struggle against (10)
Physical ___: treatment of injury by physical means rather than with drugs (7)
Reasons for disapproving or disliking (10)
Regard as perfect or more nearly perfect than is true (8)
Remove a tenant by legal procedures (5)
Restored confidence (11)
Rich, moist spongecake, often with a creamy filling between layers (7)
Shininess; brightness; luster (5)
Show respect by kneeling and touching the ground with the forehead (6)
Soft yarn used for sweaters (6)
Strong wind (4)
Tasteless (5)
Thin and weak, as from illness (6)
Trademark for a kind of weight-lifting equipment (8)
Tube inserted into the body to drain urine from the bladder (8)
Uniform worn by servants or those in some particular group or trade (6)
Widely but unfavorably known (9)
Word used to acknowledge a successful point (6)
Worn out by old age (8)

Izzy, Willy-Nilly Vocabulary Word Search 2 Answer Key

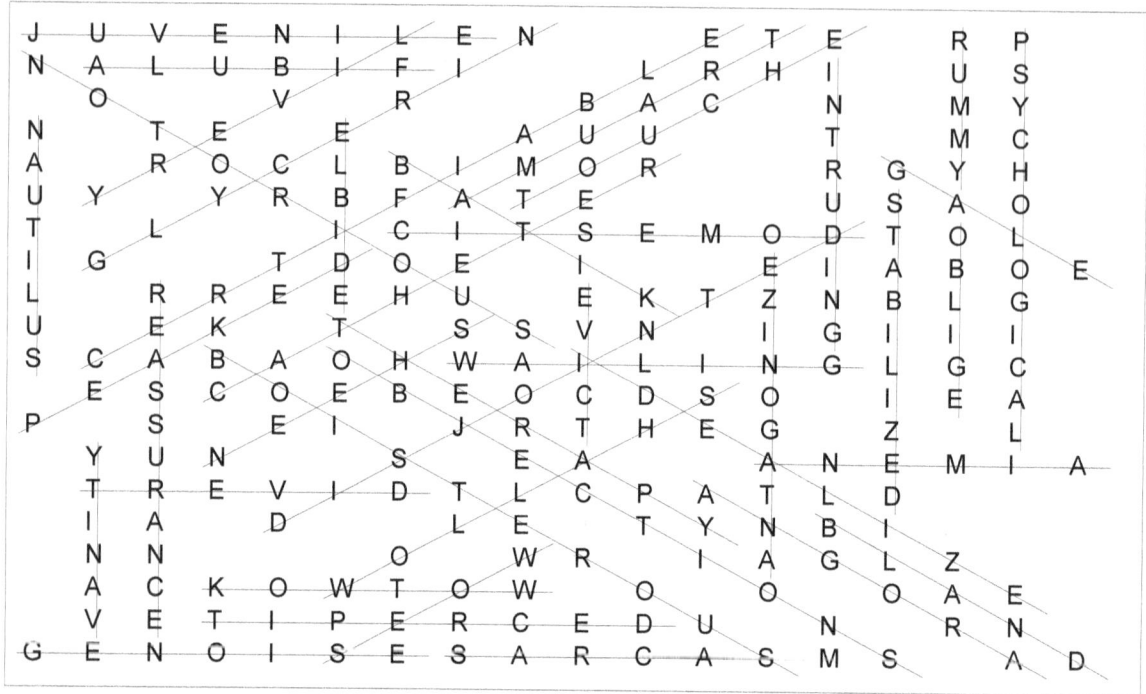

A taunting or cutting remark (7)
Anything fit to be eaten (6)
Bodily injury, wound, or shock (6)
Card game (5)
Characteristic of children (8)
Cloth decorated with dye--made by coating sections not to be dyed with removable wax (5)
Disconnected (10)
Distract the attention of (6)
Excessively proud of oneself of one's qualities or possessions (6)
Forcing oneself upon others without being asked (9)
Great sorrows or troubles (4)
Having a reduced red blood count resulting in paleness & weakness (6)
Having to do with the home or housekeeping (8)
Insane (11)
Kept from changing (10)
Lacking depth of character; superficial (7)
Long, pitiful crying (7)
Long, thin outer bone of the human leg, between the knee and ankle (6)
Noisy and lively (10)
Obligation of people of high social position to behave kindly toward others: noblesse ___ (6)
Odorless, colorless liquid used in skin lotion and other products (8)

Of the mind; mental (13)
Oppose; struggle against (10)
Physical ___: treatment of injury by physical means rather than with drugs (7)
Reasons for disapproving or disliking (10)
Regard as perfect or more nearly perfect than is true (8)
Remove a tenant by legal procedures (5)
Restored confidence (11)
Rich, moist spongecake, often with a creamy filling between layers (7)
Shininess; brightness; luster (5)
Show respect by kneeling and touching the ground with the forehead (6)
Soft yarn used for sweaters (6)
Strong wind (4)
Tasteless (5)
Thin and weak, as from illness (6)
Trademark for a kind of weight-lifting equipment (8)
Tube inserted into the body to drain urine from the bladder (8)
Uniform worn by servants or those in some particular group or trade (6)
Widely but unfavorably known (9)
Word used to acknowledge a successful point (6)
Worn out by old age (8)

Izzy, Willy-Nilly Vocabulary Word Search 3

AMPUTATED	DIVERT	KOWTOW	SHALLOW
ANEMIA	DOMESTIC	LIBERATED	SHEEN
ANGORA	DWINDLED	LIVERY	SMOLDERING
AVULSED	EDIBLE	NOTORIOUS	SOLITAIRE
BATIK	EVICT	OBJECTIONS	SUBTLETY
BLAND	FIBULA	OBLIGE	THERAPY
CATHETER	GALE	PEAKED	TOUCHE
CONDEMNED	GLYCERIN	PEROSHKIS	TRAUMA
CONJUGATIONS	GROUSED	PRECONCEPTIONS	VANITY
CONTINGENCY	ILLUSION	PROSTHETIC	WAILING
CONTUSIONS	INCOMPETENT	PSYCHOLOGICAL	WOES
CONVENIENT	INCONVENIENT	RELUCTANCE	
DIMINUTIVE	INDEFINITE	RUMMY	
DISJOINTED	INTRUDING	SARCASM	

Izzy, Willy-Nilly Vocabulary Word Search 3 Answer Key

AMPUTATED	DIVERT	KOWTOW	SHALLOW
ANEMIA	DOMESTIC	LIBERATED	SHEEN
ANGORA	DWINDLED	LIVERY	SMOLDERING
AVULSED	EDIBLE	NOTORIOUS	SOLITAIRE
BATIK	EVICT	OBJECTIONS	SUBTLETY
BLAND	FIBULA	OBLIGE	THERAPY
CATHETER	GALE	PEAKED	TOUCHE
CONDEMNED	GLYCERIN	PEROSHKIS	TRAUMA
CONJUGATIONS	GROUSED	PRECONCEPTIONS	VANITY
CONTINGENCY	ILLUSION	PROSTHETIC	WAILING
CONTUSIONS	INCOMPETENT	PSYCHOLOGICAL	WOES
CONVENIENT	INCONVENIENT	RELUCTANCE	
DIMINUTIVE	INDEFINITE	RUMMY	
DISJOINTED	INTRUDING	SARCASM	

Izzy, Willy-Nilly Vocabulary Word Search 4

```
S H A L L O W E M P H A T I C A L L Y X
I N T E N S I T Y D C W L D S E W E Q
N C V Q X V Y N D T E A A L E O D D V S
E K O W T O W E V I C T I U F L I O I T
E T T N P X L C R N R H L S L I B M T M
D N H V V D T R G A E E I I A T L E C D
L B X E N E E O L V P T N O T A E S E Y
E B O I R L N S Y H I E G N E R L T J L
P W W I E A K I C D T R S P D Y A I B Y
O D F V S Q P S E M H H O F K R X C O R
I L A G U T C Y R N E B B F E E Z L S N V
N N R L L A E O I E T B L B G T T L P V
T R E V I D M R N A I C I R T A I D E P
R C Z M T V H C O T Y L G P M I L K R T
B Y E B U G E E A U U X E U W T N E O E
P N R A A R L R P N S S A J D O L Q S P
A E I T N O I T Y Q G R I N T G E I H Q
S S A I Q U N I T D T O A O K E O S K N
P A T K C S E F Y E S L R M N N D T I C
G R I D E E V I P S B I Z A E S E B S Y
V C L Y Z D U A G L O C H G Y H Z Q K B
K A O S F B J B V U C Z L M C R M H R H
G S S X L N M L S V H P M U H N N B L N
A M P U T A T E D A X U O F I B U L A J
B A N K R U P T C Y R T I D E A L I Z E
```

AMPUTATED CONVENIENT GENOISE NAUTILUS SARCASM

ANEMIA DECREPIT GLYCERIN NECROSIS SHALLOW

ANGORA DEFLATED GROUSED NEEDLEPOINT SHEEN

AVULSED DIVERT IDEALIZE NEGOTIATE SOLITAIRE

BANKRUPTCY DOMESTIC ILLUSION NOTORIOUS SOLITARY

BATIK DWINDLED INTENSITY OBJECTIVE THERAPY

BLAND EDIBLE IRRELEVANT OBLIGE TOUCHE

BOISTEROUS EMPHATICALLY JUVENILE PEAKED TRAUMA

CATHETER EVICT KOWTOW PEDIATRICIAN VANITY

CERTIFIABLE FIBULA LIBERATED PEROSHKIS WAILING

CONTUSIONS GALE LIVERY RUMMY WOES

Izzy, Willy-Nilly Vocabulary Word Search 4 Answer Key

```
S H A L L O W E M P H A T I C A L L Y
I N T E N S I T Y Y D C W D S E E
N C     N D T E A L D O D V
E K O W T O W E V R N T I L E I I
E T N   L C G A T H U L D M T
D   H V D R L V E T S I A E C
L B E N E E O Y P T R I T L S E
E O I R L N S I E H O A E T J
P W R E A   C   R   N D R   I B
O D V S U T P N E   B E   C O
I   A L T A S C R T L G T
N N E I V E O I A   I R A I P
T R V D D R C N C   E M L D E E
    M T V   E O T U   U W T N O P
P   E B U G E   R U S G T   E O R
A N R A A R L   N S A T G   S O
  E I T N O I   Y D R O N E I S
  S A T K   U E     E L A N N   K H
  A T I   E S V   S B G Y S   I K
  R C L K   E I       O M C   S I
  C A O     D U A     U   M U     S
  A S S       J B       F   A
A M P U T A T E D A   U O F I B U L A
B A N K R U P T C Y R T I D E A L I Z E
```

AMPUTATED	CONVENIENT	GENOISE	NAUTILUS	SARCASM
ANEMIA	DECREPIT	GLYCERIN	NECROSIS	SHALLOW
ANGORA	DEFLATED	GROUSED	NEEDLEPOINT	SHEEN
AVULSED	DIVERT	IDEALIZE	NEGOTIATE	SOLITAIRE
BANKRUPTCY	DOMESTIC	ILLUSION	NOTORIOUS	SOLITARY
BATIK	DWINDLED	INTENSITY	OBJECTIVE	THERAPY
BLAND	EDIBLE	IRRELEVANT	OBLIGE	TOUCHE
BOISTEROUS	EMPHATICALLY	JUVENILE	PEAKED	TRAUMA
CATHETER	EVICT	KOWTOW	PEDIATRICIAN	VANITY
CERTIFIABLE	FIBULA	LIBERATED	PEROSHKIS	WAILING
CONTUSIONS	GALE	LIVERY	RUMMY	WOES

Izzy, Willy-Nilly Vocabulary Crossword 1

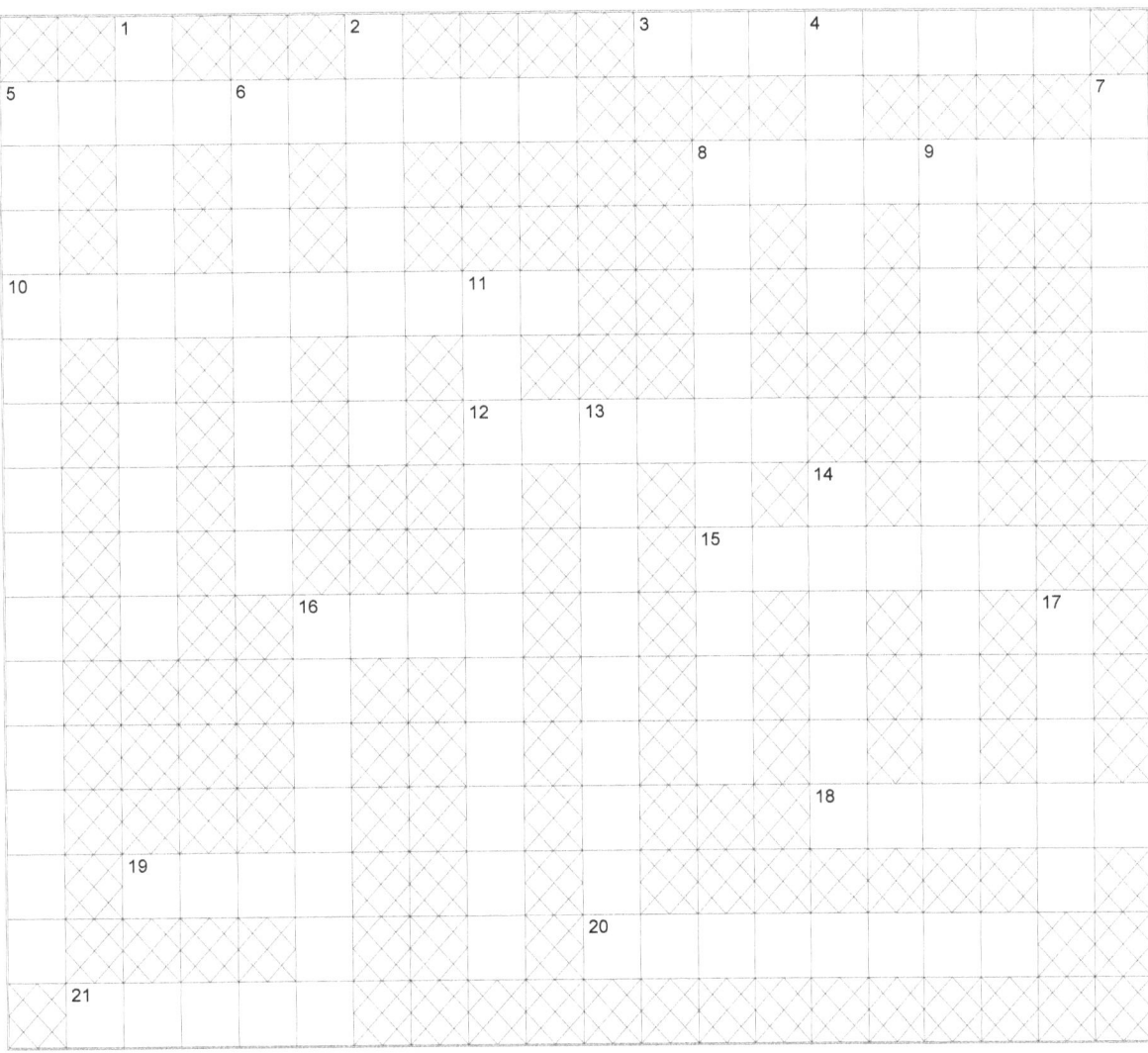

Across
3. Bragging
5. Having a right, advantage, or favor that is withheld from certain or all others
8. Regard as perfect or more nearly perfect than is true
10. Bruises
12. Anything fit to be eaten
15. Excessively proud of oneself of one's qualities or possessions
16. Strong wind
18. Having a reduced red blood count resulting in paleness & weakness
19. Great sorrows or troubles
20. Odorless, colorless liquid used in skin lotion and other products
21. Tasteless

Down
1. Very small
2. Rich, moist spongecake, often with a creamy filling between layers
4. Shininess; brightness; luster
5. Opinions formed in advance
6. False perception of what one sees
7. Thin and weak, as from illness
8. Not pertinent; not having anything to do with the matter at hand
9. Rich pastry made of almond dough & raspberry jam filling
11. Embroidery of threads upon a canvas
13. Forcing oneself upon others without being asked
14. Soft yarn used for sweaters
16. Grumbled
17. Cloth decorated with dye--made by coating sections not to be dyed with removable wax

Izzy, Willy-Nilly Vocabulary Crossword 1 Answer Key

	1 D		2 G		3 B	O	A	4 S	T	I	N	G	
5 P	R	I	V	6 I	L	E	G	E	D				7 P
R	M	I	L	N			8 I	D	E	A	9 L	I	Z	E
R	I	L	O				R	E	I		A
10 C	O	N	T	U	S	I	O	11 N	S		R	N	N	K
O	U	S	S	E			E	Z	E
N	T	I	S	12 E	13 D	I	B	L	E		E	D
C	I	O	D	N	E	14 A	R
E	V	N	L	T	15 V	A	N	I	T	Y
P	E	16 G	A	L	E	R	A	G	O	17 B
T	R	P	U	N	O	R	A
I	O	O	D	T	R	T	T
O	U	I	I	18 A	N	E	M	I	A
N	19 W	O	E	S	N	N	K
S	E	T	20 G	L	Y	C	E	R	I	N
21 B	L	A	N	D

Across
3. Bragging
5. Having a right, advantage, or favor that is withheld from certain or all others
8. Regard as perfect or more nearly perfect than is true
10. Bruises
12. Anything fit to be eaten
15. Excessively proud of oneself of one's qualities or possessions
16. Strong wind
18. Having a reduced red blood count resulting in paleness & weakness
19. Great sorrows or troubles
20. Odorless, colorless liquid used in skin lotion and other products
21. Tasteless

Down
1. Very small
2. Rich, moist spongecake, often with a creamy filling between layers
4. Shininess; brightness; luster
5. Opinions formed in advance
6. False perception of what one sees
7. Thin and weak, as from illness
8. Not pertinent; not having anything to do with the matter at hand
9. Rich pastry made of almond dough & raspberry jam filling
11. Embroidery of threads upon a canvas
13. Forcing oneself upon others without being asked
14. Soft yarn used for sweaters
16. Grumbled
17. Cloth decorated with dye--made by coating sections not to be dyed with removable wax

Izzy, Willy-Nilly Vocabulary Crossword 2

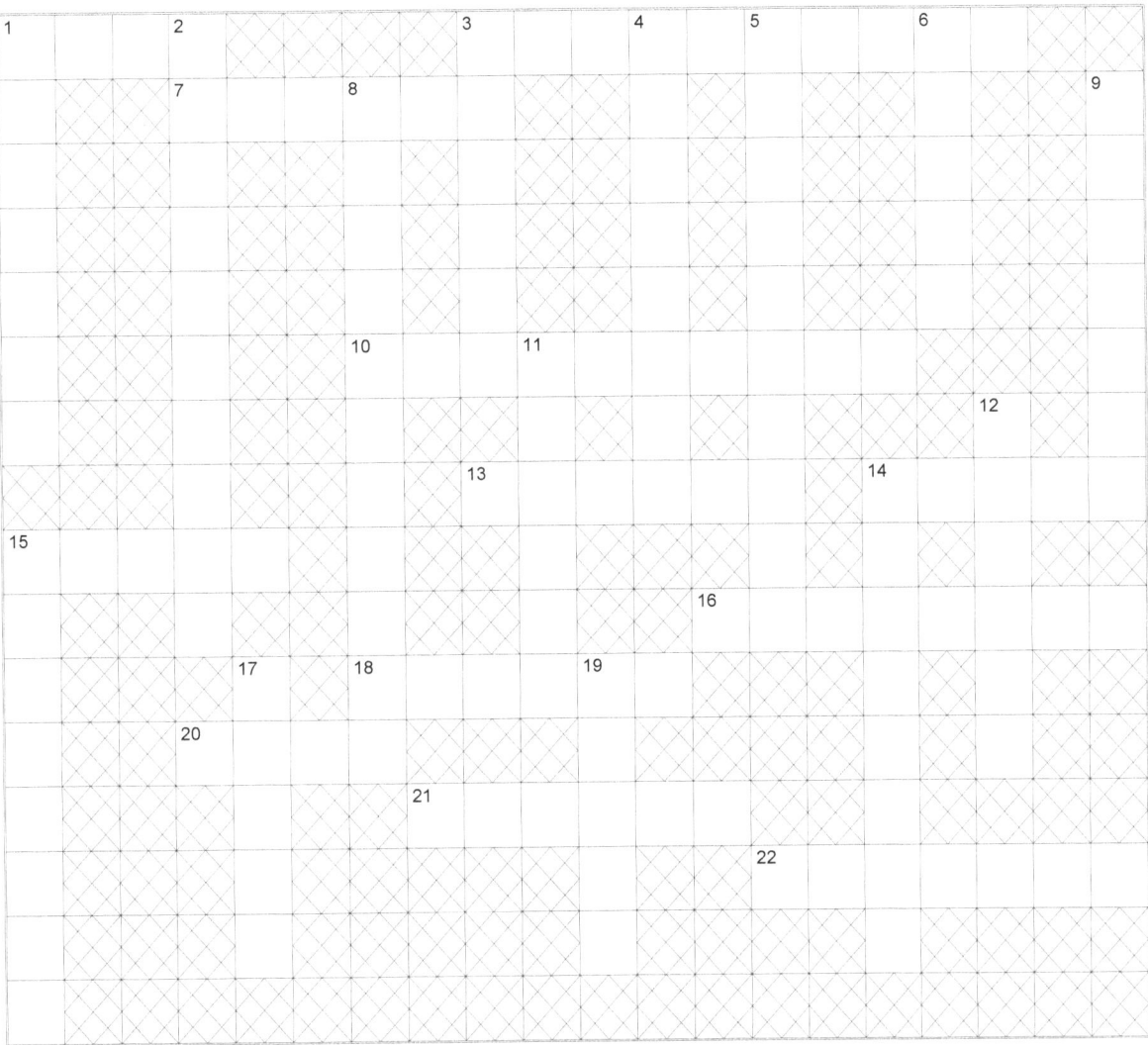

Across
1. Great sorrows or troubles
3. Suspicion, intolerance, or irrational hatred of certain others
7. Word used to acknowledge a successful point
10. Not precise or clear in meaning; vague
13. Distract the attention of
14. Tasteless
15. Shininess; brightness; luster
16. Regard as perfect or more nearly perfect than is true
18. Uniform worn by servants or those in some particular group or trade
20. Strong wind
21. Having a reduced red blood count resulting in paleness & weakness
22. Rich, moist spongecake, often with a creamy filling between layers

Down
1. Long, pitiful crying
2. Kept from changing
3. Thin and weak, as from illness
4. Characteristic of children
5. Disconnected
6. Remove a tenant by legal procedures
8. Insane
9. Grumbled
11. Anything fit to be eaten
12. Excessively proud of oneself of one's qualities or possessions
14. Bragging
15. Ability to be delicately suggestive
17. Cloth decorated with dye--made by coating sections not to be dyed with removable wax
19. Card game

Izzy, Willy-Nilly Vocabulary Crossword 2 Answer Key

Across
1. Great sorrows or troubles
3. Suspicion, intolerance, or irrational hatred of certain others
7. Word used to acknowledge a successful point
10. Not precise or clear in meaning; vague
13. Distract the attention of
14. Tasteless
15. Shininess; brightness; luster
16. Regard as perfect or more nearly perfect than is true
18. Uniform worn by servants or those in some particular group or trade
20. Strong wind
21. Having a reduced red blood count resulting in paleness & weakness
22. Rich, moist spongecake, often with a creamy filling between layers

Down
1. Long, pitiful crying
2. Kept from changing
3. Thin and weak, as from illness
4. Characteristic of children
5. Disconnected
6. Remove a tenant by legal procedures
8. Insane
9. Grumbled
11. Anything fit to be eaten
12. Excessively proud of oneself of one's qualities or possessions
14. Bragging
15. Ability to be delicately suggestive
17. Cloth decorated with dye--made by coating sections not to be dyed with removable wax
19. Card game

Copyrighted

Izzy, Willy-Nilly Vocabulary Crossword 3

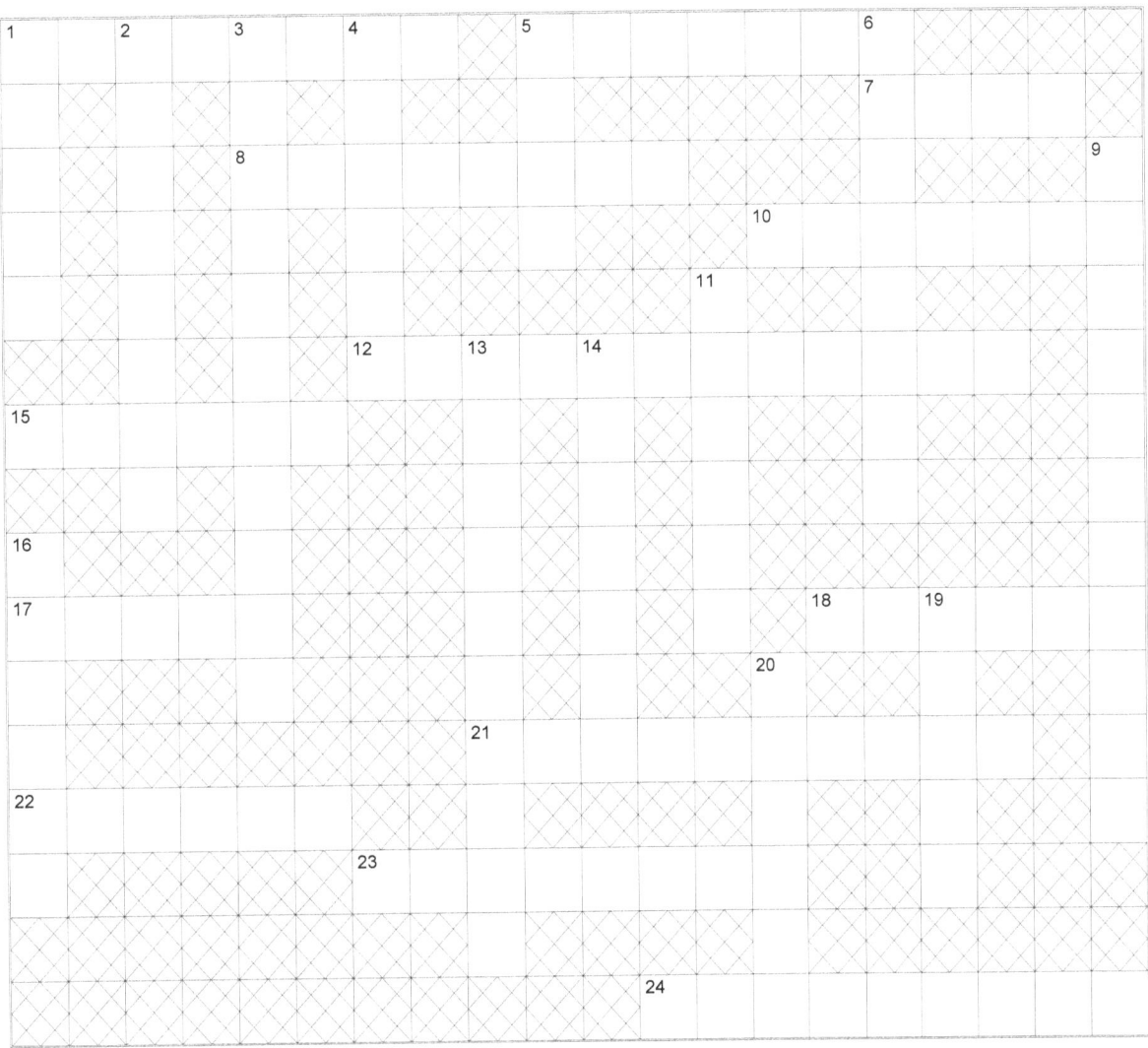

Across
1. Ability to be delicately suggestive
5. Grumbled
7. Great sorrows or troubles
8. Trademark for a kind of weight-lifting equipment
10. Rich, moist spongecake, often with a creamy filling between layers
12. Done with emphasis or strength
15. Excessively proud of oneself of one's qualities or possessions
17. Remove a tenant by legal procedures
18. Long, thin outer bone of the human leg, between the knee and ankle
21. Not precise or clear in meaning; vague
22. Anything fit to be eaten
23. Regard as perfect or more nearly perfect than is true
24. Forcing oneself upon others without being asked

Down
1. Shininess; brightness; luster
2. Bragging
3. Rich pastry made of almond dough & raspberry jam filling
4. Word used to acknowledge a successful point
5. Strong wind
6. Diminished; made less
9. Insane
11. Uniform worn by servants or those in some particular group or trade
13. Suspicion, intolerance, or irrational hatred of certain others
14. Tore away by surgical traction
16. Thin and weak, as from illness
19. Cloth decorated with dye--made by coating sections not to be dyed with removable wax
20. Distract the attention of

Izzy, Willy-Nilly Vocabulary Crossword 3 Answer Key

	1 S	U	2 B	T	3 L	E	4 T	Y		5 G	R	O	U	S	E	6 D	
	H		O		I		O			A						7 W	O E S
	E		A		8 N	A	U	T	I	L	U	S				I	
	E		S		Z		C			E			10 G	E	N	O I S E
	N		T		E		H		11 L				D				R
			I		R		12 E	13 M	14 P	H	A	T	I	C	A	L	L Y	T
15 V	A	N	I	T	Y			R		V		V		A		L		I
			G		O			E		U		E		D				F
16 P			R					J		L		R						I
17 E	V	I	C	T				U		S		Y		18 F	I	19 B	U L A
A			E					D		E			20 D			A		B
K							21 I	N	D	E	F	I	N	I	T	E		L
22 E	D	I	B	L	E		C						V			I		E
D						23 I	D	E	A	L	I	Z	E			K		
							S						R					
												24 I	N	T	R	U	D I N G

Across

1. Ability to be delicately suggestive
5. Grumbled
7. Great sorrows or troubles
8. Trademark for a kind of weight-lifting equipment
10. Rich, moist spongecake, often with a creamy filling between layers
12. Done with emphasis or strength
15. Excessively proud of oneself of one's qualities or possessions
17. Remove a tenant by legal procedures
18. Long, thin outer bone of the human leg, between the knee and ankle
21. Not precise or clear in meaning; vague
22. Anything fit to be eaten
23. Regard as perfect or more nearly perfect than is true
24. Forcing oneself upon others without being asked

Down

1. Shininess; brightness; luster
2. Bragging
3. Rich pastry made of almond dough & raspberry jam filling
4. Word used to acknowledge a successful point
5. Strong wind
6. Diminished; made less
9. Insane
11. Uniform worn by servants or those in some particular group or trade
13. Suspicion, intolerance, or irrational hatred of certain others
14. Tore away by surgical traction
16. Thin and weak, as from illness
19. Cloth decorated with dye--made by coating sections not to be dyed with removable wax
20. Distract the attention of

Izzy, Willy-Nilly Vocabulary Crossword 4

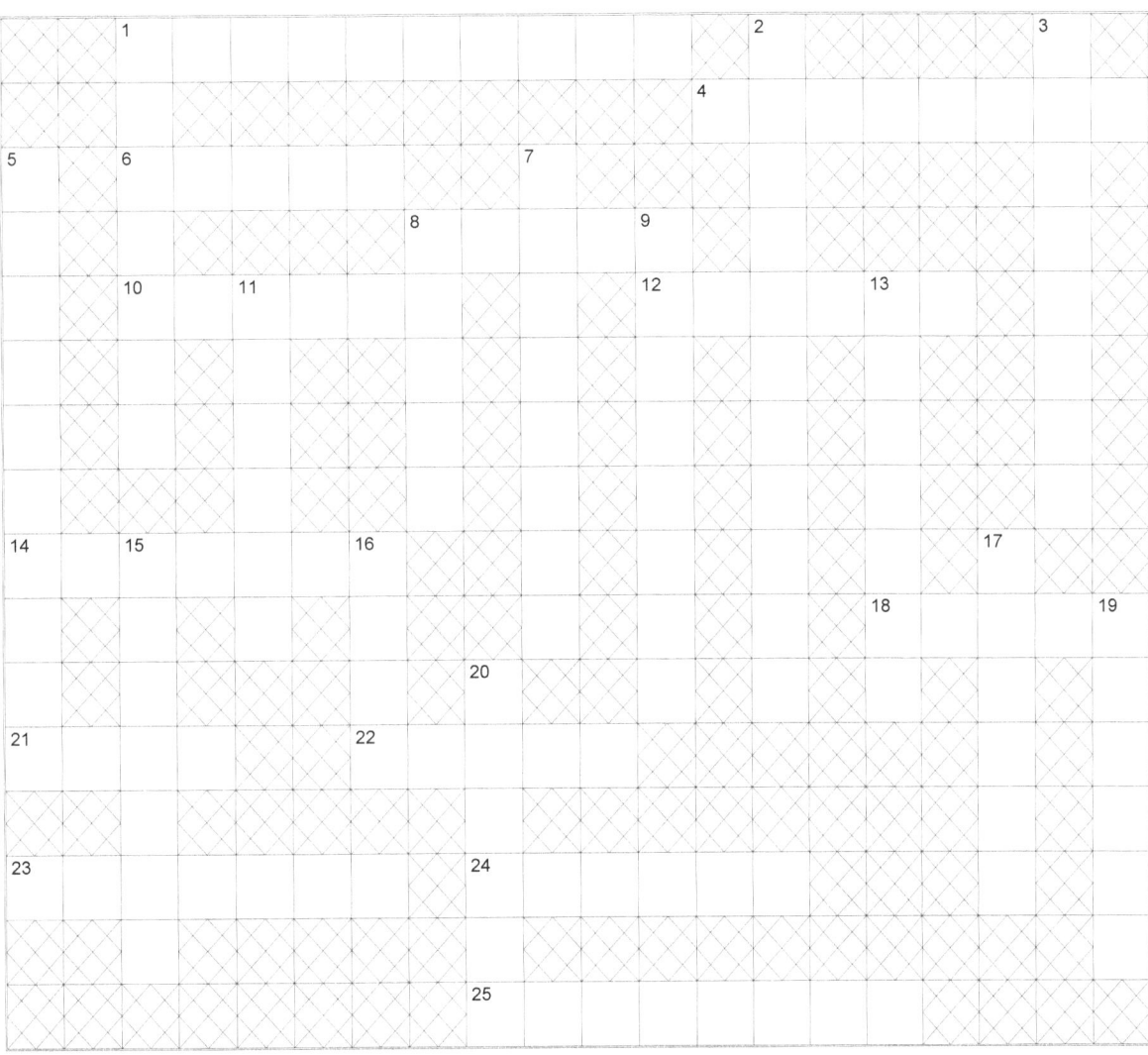

Across
1. Burning
4. Characteristic of children
6. Card game
8. Tasteless
10. Having a reduced red blood count resulting in paleness & weakness
12. Obligation of people of high social position to behave kindly toward others: noblesse ___
14. Lacking depth of character; superficial
18. Remove a tenant by legal procedures
21. Strong wind
22. Shininess; brightness; luster
23. Physical ___: treatment of injury by physical means rather than with drugs
24. Show respect by kneeling and touching the ground with the forehead
25. Worn out by old age

Down
1. A taunting or cutting remark
2. Feeling hurt pride or dignity being or seeming foolish
3. Odorless, colorless liquid used in skin lotion and other products
5. Holding back
7. Trademark for a kind of weight-lifting equipment
8. Cloth decorated with dye--made by coating sections not to be dyed with removable wax
9. Having to do with the home or housekeeping
11. Anything fit to be eaten
13. Grumbled
15. Tore away by surgical traction
16. Great sorrows or troubles
17. Distract the attention of
19. Word used to acknowledge a successful point
20. Thin and weak, as from illness

Izzy, Willy-Nilly Vocabulary Crossword 4 Answer Key

	1 S	M	O	L	D	E	R	I	N	G		2 H					3 G
	A								4 J	U	V	E	N	I	L	E
5 R	6 R	U	M	M	Y		7 N			M					Y	
E	C					8 B	L	A	N	9 D		I				C
P	10 A	N	11 E	M	I	A		U		12 O	B	L	I	13 G	E	E
R		S		D		T		T		M		I		R		R
E				I		I		I		E		A		O		I
S				B		K		L		S		T		U		N
14 S	H	15 A	L	L	16 O	W		U		T		I		S	17 D	
I		V		E	O			S		I		O	18 E	V	I	C	19 T
N		U			E	20 P		C		N		D		V		O
21 G	A	L	E		22 S	H	E	E	N				E		U
		S				A							R		C
23 T	H	E	R	A	P	Y	24 K	O	W	T	O	W		T		H
		D				E										E
					25 D	E	C	R	E	P	I	T				

Across
1. Burning
4. Characteristic of children
6. Card game
8. Tasteless
10. Having a reduced red blood count resulting in paleness & weakness
12. Obligation of people of high social position to behave kindly toward others: noblesse ___
14. Lacking depth of character; superficial
18. Remove a tenant by legal procedures
21. Strong wind
22. Shininess; brightness; luster
23. Physical ___: treatment of injury by physical means rather than with drugs
24. Show respect by kneeling and touching the ground with the forehead
25. Worn out by old age

Down
1. A taunting or cutting remark
2. Feeling hurt pride or dignity being or seeming foolish
3. Odorless, colorless liquid used in skin lotion and other products
5. Holding back
7. Trademark for a kind of weight-lifting equipment
8. Cloth decorated with dye--made by coating sections not to be dyed with removable wax
9. Having to do with the home or housekeeping
11. Anything fit to be eaten
13. Grumbled
15. Tore away by surgical traction
16. Great sorrows or troubles
17. Distract the attention of
19. Word used to acknowledge a successful point
20. Thin and weak, as from illness

Izzy, Willy-Nilly Vocabulary Juggle Letters 1

1. EPYATRH = 1. _____
   Physical ___: treatment of injury by physical means rather than with drugs

2. AITIOLERS = 2. _____
   Card game played by one person

3. DIEBEL = 3. _____
   Anything fit to be eaten

4. GNUNTIIRD = 4. _____
   Forcing oneself upon others without being asked

5. OOSTIURNO = 5. _____
   Widely but unfavorably known

6. YOGASCCLIOLHP = 6. _____
   Of the mind; mental

7. HRTCTEAE = 7. _____
   Tube inserted into the body to drain urine from the bladder

8. ALIUNTSU = 8. _____
   Trademark for a kind of weight-lifting equipment

9. OSLNIDGMER = 9. _____
   Burning

10. ICTDPIAAERIN =10. _____
    Medical doctor specializing in the care of children

11. AHOLLSW =11. _____
    Lacking depth of character; superficial

12. EHOCUT =12. _____
    Word used to acknowledge a successful point

13. GELPVIDIER =13. _____
    Having a right, advantage, or favor that is withheld from certain or all others

14. TEVCBIJOE =14. _____
    Without bias or prejudice

15. DIEEINTNIF =15. _____
    Not precise or clear in meaning; vague

Izzy, Willy-Nilly Vocabulary Juggle Letters 1 Answer Key

1. EPYATRH = 1. THERAPY
Physical ___: treatment of injury by physical means rather than with drugs

2. AITIOLERS = 2. SOLITAIRE
Card game played by one person

3. DIEBEL = 3. EDIBLE
Anything fit to be eaten

4. GNUNTIIRD = 4. INTRUDING
Forcing oneself upon others without being asked

5. OOSTIURNO = 5. NOTORIOUS
Widely but unfavorably known

6. YOGASCCLIOLHP = 6. PSYCHOLOGICAL
Of the mind; mental

7. HRTCTEAE = 7. CATHETER
Tube inserted into the body to drain urine from the bladder

8. ALIUNTSU = 8. NAUTILUS
Trademark for a kind of weight-lifting equipment

9. OSLNIDGMER = 9. SMOLDERING
Burning

10. ICTDPIAAERIN = 10. PEDIATRICIAN
Medical doctor specializing in the care of children

11. AHOLLSW = 11. SHALLOW
Lacking depth of character; superficial

12. EHOCUT = 12. TOUCHE
Word used to acknowledge a successful point

13. GELPVIDIER = 13. PRIVILEGED
Having a right, advantage, or favor that is withheld from certain or all others

14. TEVCBIJOE = 14. OBJECTIVE
Without bias or prejudice

15. DIEEINTNIF = 15. INDEFINITE
Not precise or clear in meaning; vague

Izzy, Willy-Nilly Vocabulary Juggle Letters 2

1. EINVCTOENN = 1. _____
   Easy to do, use or get to; easily accessible

2. NGNEYINTCCO = 2. _____
   A possible, unforeseen, or accidental occurrence

3. OTKOWW = 3. _____
   Show respect by kneeling and touching the ground with the forehead

4. DLWDDEIN = 4. _____
   Diminished; made less

5. EINDUVTMII = 5. _____
   Very small

6. UTDMTAPEA = 6. _____
   Cut off through surgery

7. DNNEEUIDTR = 7. _____
   ____ servant: one who is (voluntarily or not) committed to working for someone for a number of years

8. ITCEV = 8. _____
   Remove a tenant by legal procedures

9. ERSSEGPRIN = 9. _____
   Holding back

10. IRTVDE =10. _____
    Distract the attention of

11. LAIZEIED =11. _____
    Regard as perfect or more nearly perfect than is true

12. IAMANE =12. _____
    Having a reduced red blood count resulting in paleness & weakness

13. ESMIDCTO =13. _____
    Having to do with the home or housekeeping

14. THATEERC =14. _____
    Tube inserted into the body to drain urine from the bladder

15. ILETZNTRORE =15. _____
    Rich pastry made of almond dough & raspberry jam filling

Izzy, Willy-Nilly Vocabulary Juggle Letters 2 Answer Key

1. EINVCTOENN = 1. CONVENIENT
   Easy to do, use or get to; easily accessible

2. NGNEYINTCCO = 2. CONTINGENCY
   A possible, unforeseen, or accidental occurrence

3. OTKOWW = 3. KOWTOW
   Show respect by kneeling and touching the ground with the forehead

4. DLWDDEIN = 4. DWINDLED
   Diminished; made less

5. EINDUVTMII = 5. DIMINUTIVE
   Very small

6. UTDMTAPEA = 6. AMPUTATED
   Cut off through surgery

7. DNNEEUIDTR = 7. INDENTURED
   ____ servant: one who is (voluntarily or not) committed to working for someone for a number of years

8. ITCEV = 8. EVICT
   Remove a tenant by legal procedures

9. ERSSEGPRIN = 9. REPRESSING
   Holding back

10. IRTVDE = 10. DIVERT
    Distract the attention of

11. LAIZEIED = 11. IDEALIZE
    Regard as perfect or more nearly perfect than is true

12. IAMANE = 12. ANEMIA
    Having a reduced red blood count resulting in paleness & weakness

13. ESMIDCTO = 13. DOMESTIC
    Having to do with the home or housekeeping

14. THATEERC = 14. CATHETER
    Tube inserted into the body to drain urine from the bladder

15. ILETZNTRORE = 15. LINZERTORTE
    Rich pastry made of almond dough & raspberry jam filling

Izzy, Willy-Nilly Vocabulary Juggle Letters 3

1. EIDLPVERGI = 1. _____
Having a right, advantage, or favor that is withheld from certain or all others

2. SOILARYT = 2. _____
Being alone

3. EEDDURTNIN = 3. _____
____ servant: one who is (voluntarily or not) committed to working for someone for a number of years

4. UJINEVLE = 4. _____
Characteristic of children

5. TEIMIDVINU = 5. _____
Very small

6. LMINIAOUHTI = 6. _____
Feeling hurt pride or dignity being or seeming foolish

7. EIERTRPEOR = 7. _____
Special skills, techniques, etc. of a particular person

8. UALBFI = 8. _____
Long, thin outer bone of the human leg, between the knee and ankle

9. ONJOANTSUICG = 9. _____
Inflectional forms of verbs

10. ENMCENPIOTT = 10. _____
Incapable; unskilled

11. VNEONINTCE = 11. _____
Easy to do, use or get to; easily accessible

12. CUHTEO = 12. _____
Word used to acknowledge a successful point

13. DILNEDWD = 13. _____
Diminished; made less

14. GNRPIESSRE = 14. _____
Holding back

15. AEKPED = 15. _____
Thin and weak, as from illness

Izzy, Willy-Nilly Vocabulary Juggle Letters 3 Answer Key

1. EIDLPVERGI = 1. PRIVILEGED
Having a right, advantage, or favor that is withheld from certain or all others

2. SOILARYT = 2. SOLITARY
Being alone

3. EEDDURTNIN = 3. INDENTURED
____ servant: one who is (voluntarily or not) committed to working for someone for a number of years

4. UJINEVLE = 4. JUVENILE
Characteristic of children

5. TEIMIDVINU = 5. DIMINUTIVE
Very small

6. LMINIAOUHTI = 6. HUMILIATION
Feeling hurt pride or dignity being or seeming foolish

7. EIERTRPEOR = 7. REPERTOIRE
Special skills, techniques, etc. of a particular person

8. UALBFI = 8. FIBULA
Long, thin outer bone of the human leg, between the knee and ankle

9. ONJOANTSUICG = 9. CONJUGATIONS
Inflectional forms of verbs

10. ENMCENPIOTT =10. INCOMPETENT
Incapable; unskilled

11. VNEONINTCE =11. CONVENIENT
Easy to do, use or get to; easily accessible

12. CUHTEO =12. TOUCHE
Word used to acknowledge a successful point

13. DILNEDWD =13. DWINDLED
Diminished; made less

14. GNRPIESSRE =14. REPRESSING
Holding back

15. AEKPED =15. PEAKED
Thin and weak, as from illness

Izzy, Willy-Nilly Vocabulary Juggle Letters 4

1. EEATIRBDL = 1. _____
   Set free; released

2. ZAILEDEI = 2. _____
   Regard as perfect or more nearly perfect than is true

3. CARSAMS = 3. _____
   A taunting or cutting remark

4. OJNGCSTIUOAN = 4. _____
   Inflectional forms of verbs

5. AUADPTTEM = 5. _____
   Cut off through surgery

6. PDETEIRC = 6. _____
   Worn out by old age

7. SNTNSUIOCO = 7. _____
   Bruises

8. MUARAT = 8. _____
   Bodily injury, wound, or shock

9. UDEDNRINET = 9. _____
   ____ servant: one who is (voluntarily or not) committed to working for someone for a number of years

10. PHETMLICYAAL =10. _____
    Done with emphasis or strength

11. AAGRON =11. _____
    Soft yarn used for sweaters

12. HLWOSAL =12. _____
    Lacking depth of character; superficial

13. OURDGES =13. _____
    Grumbled

14. OLTEREITRZN =14. _____
    Rich pastry made of almond dough & raspberry jam filling

15. NDODMNEEC =15. _____
    Disapproved of strongly

Izzy, Willy-Nilly Vocabulary Juggle Letters 4 Answer Key

1. EEATIRBDL = 1. LIBERATED
   Set free; released

2. ZAILEDEI = 2. IDEALIZE
   Regard as perfect or more nearly perfect than is true

3. CARSAMS = 3. SARCASM
   A taunting or cutting remark

4. OJNGCSTIUOAN = 4. CONJUGATIONS
   Inflectional forms of verbs

5. AUADPTTEM = 5. AMPUTATED
   Cut off through surgery

6. PDETEIRC = 6. DECREPIT
   Worn out by old age

7. SNTNSUIOCO = 7. CONTUSIONS
   Bruises

8. MUARAT = 8. TRAUMA
   Bodily injury, wound, or shock

9. UDEDNRINET = 9. INDENTURED
   ____ servant: one who is (voluntarily or not) committed to working for someone for a number of years

10. PHETMLICYAAL = 10. EMPHATICALLY
    Done with emphasis or strength

11. AAGRON = 11. ANGORA
    Soft yarn used for sweaters

12. HLWOSAL = 12. SHALLOW
    Lacking depth of character; superficial

13. OURDGES = 13. GROUSED
    Grumbled

14. OLTEREITRZN = 14. LINZERTORTE
    Rich pastry made of almond dough & raspberry jam filling

15. NDODMNEEC = 15. CONDEMNED
    Disapproved of strongly

Copyrighted

AMPUTATED	Cut off through surgery
ANEMIA	Having a reduced red blood count resulting in paleness & weakness
ANGORA	Soft yarn used for sweaters
ANTAGONIZE	Oppose; struggle against
AVULSED	Tore away by surgical traction

BANKRUPTCY	State of being unable to pay debts
BATIK	Cloth decorated with dye--made by coating sections not to be dyed with removable wax
BLAND	Tasteless
BOASTING	Bragging
BOISTEROUS	Noisy and lively

CATHETER	Tube inserted into the body to drain urine from the bladder
CERTIFIABLE	Insane
CONDEMNED	Disapproved of strongly
CONJUGATIONS	Inflectional forms of verbs
CONTINGENCY	A possible, unforeseen, or accidental occurrence

CONTUSIONS	Bruises
CONVENIENT	Easy to do, use or get to; easily accessible
DECREPIT	Worn out by old age
DEFLATED	Made smaller or less important
DIMINUTIVE	Very small

DISJOINTED	Disconnected
DIVERSIONARY	Serving to distract the attention
DIVERT	Distract the attention of
DOMESTIC	Having to do with the home or housekeeping
DWINDLED	Diminished; made less

EDIBLE	Anything fit to be eaten
EMPHATICALLY	Done with emphasis or strength
EVICT	Remove a tenant by legal procedures
FIBULA	Long, thin outer bone of the human leg, between the knee and ankle
GALE	Strong wind

GENOISE	Rich, moist spongecake, often with a creamy filling between layers
GLYCERIN	Odorless, colorless liquid used in skin lotion and other products
GROUSED	Grumbled
HUMILIATION	Feeling hurt pride or dignity being or seeming foolish
IDEALIZE	Regard as perfect or more nearly perfect than is true

ILLUSION	False perception of what one sees
INADVERTENTLY	Unintentionally; without meaning to
INCOMPETENT	Incapable; unskilled
INCONVENIENT	Not favorable to one's comfort; difficult to do
INDEFINITE	Not precise or clear in meaning; vague

INDENTURED	____ servant: one who is (voluntarily or not) committed to working for someone for a number of years
INTENSITY	Great energy of emotion, thought, or activity
INTRUDING	Forcing oneself upon others without being asked
IRRELEVANT	Not pertinent; not having anything to do with the matter at hand
JUVENILE	Characteristic of children

KOWTOW	Show respect by kneeling and touching the ground with the forehead
LIBERATED	Set free; released
LINZERTORTE	Rich pastry made of almond dough & raspberry jam filling
LIVERY	Uniform worn by servants or those in some particular group or trade
MARINATING	Soaking meat or fish in a mixture of spices or liquids prior to cooking

NAUTILUS	Trademark for a kind of weight-lifting equipment
NECROSIS	Death of decay of tissue in a part of the body
NEEDLEPOINT	Embroidery of threads upon a canvas
NEGOTIATE	Bargain or discuss in order to reach an agreement
NOTORIOUS	Widely but unfavorably known

OBJECTIONS	Reasons for disapproving or disliking
OBJECTIVE	Without bias or prejudice
OBLIGE	Obligation of people of high social position to behave kindly toward others: noblesse ___
PEAKED	Thin and weak, as from illness
PEDIATRICIAN	Medical doctor specializing in the care of children

PEROSHKIS	Small pastry turnovers with a filling
PRECONCEPTIONS	Opinions formed in advance
PREJUDICES	Suspicion, intolerance, or irrational hatred of certain others
PRIVILEGED	Having a right, advantage, or favor that is withheld from certain or all others
PROSTHETIC	Artificial replacement part of the body

PSYCHOLOGICAL	Of the mind; mental
REASSURANCE	Restored confidence
RELUCTANCE	Unwillingness
REPERTOIRE	Special skills, techniques, etc. of a particular person
REPRESSING	Holding back

RUMMY	Card game
SARCASM	A taunting or cutting remark
SHALLOW	Lacking depth of character; superficial
SHEEN	Shininess; brightness; luster
SMOLDERING	Burning

SOLITAIRE	Card game played by one person
SOLITARY	Being alone
STABILIZED	Kept from changing
SUBTLETY	Ability to be delicately suggestive
THERAPY	Physical ___: treatment of injury by physical means rather than with drugs

TOUCHE	Word used to acknowledge a successful point
TRAUMA	Bodily injury, wound, or shock
UNDERESTIMATES	Sets too low of an estimate or judgement
VANITY	Excessively proud of oneself of one's qualities or possessions
WAILING	Long, pitiful crying

WOES | Great sorrows or troubles

Izzy, Willy-Nilly Vocabulary

ANGORA	CATHETER	GLYCERIN	SHALLOW	PREJUDICES
EVICT	DEFLATED	PEROSHKIS	CONVENIENT	JUVENILE
SOLITARY	STABILIZED	FREE SPACE	IRRELEVANT	BLAND
GROUSED	DIVERT	DECREPIT	CONTINGENCY	RUMMY
PSYCHOLOGICAL	INDEFINITE	BANKRUPTCY	AMPUTATED	REASSURANCE

Izzy, Willy-Nilly Vocabulary

DISJOINTED	SMOLDERING	NAUTILUS	UNDERESTIMATES	EDIBLE
ILLUSION	NECROSIS	CONTUSIONS	OBJECTIVE	KOWTOW
INDENTURED	SHEEN	FREE SPACE	CONJUGATIONS	BOISTEROUS
GALE	PEAKED	REPERTOIRE	LIBERATED	PRECONCEPTIONS
CONDEMNED	LIVERY	NEGOTIATE	SUBTLETY	NEEDLEPOINT

Izzy, Willy-Nilly Vocabulary

MARINATING	PEAKED	PRIVILEGED	REPERTOIRE	CONJUGATIONS
PEROSHKIS	IDEALIZE	INCOMPETENT	INDENTURED	LIVERY
NEEDLEPOINT	NEGOTIATE	FREE SPACE	PREJUDICES	GENOISE
SUBTLETY	CONDEMNED	DOMESTIC	CERTIFIABLE	TOUCHE
OBJECTIVE	BLAND	LIBERATED	RELUCTANCE	CATHETER

Izzy, Willy-Nilly Vocabulary

HUMILIATION	NOTORIOUS	GLYCERIN	SOLITAIRE	GALE
SMOLDERING	INTENSITY	PROSTHETIC	SHALLOW	KOWTOW
REASSURANCE	IRRELEVANT	FREE SPACE	INTRUDING	ANTAGONIZE
DECREPIT	PEDIATRICIAN	BATIK	BANKRUPTCY	SHEEN
EVICT	NAUTILUS	WAILING	EMPHATICALLY	CONTUSIONS

Izzy, Willy-Nilly Vocabulary

VANITY	DWINDLED	INDEFINITE	PSYCHOLOGICAL	DISJOINTED
SHALLOW	PREJUDICES	NAUTILUS	GALE	INCOMPETENT
PEDIATRICIAN	SOLITARY	FREE SPACE	ANTAGONIZE	SOLITAIRE
GENOISE	OBLIGE	DIMINUTIVE	NOTORIOUS	STABILIZED
DEFLATED	ANGORA	UNDERESTIMATES	INTRUDING	ILLUSION

Izzy, Willy-Nilly Vocabulary

TOUCHE	DIVERSIONARY	PRECONCEPTIONS	NECROSIS	CONVENIENT
EVICT	EDIBLE	WAILING	BOISTEROUS	PEAKED
NEGOTIATE	RELUCTANCE	FREE SPACE	GROUSED	SUBTLETY
PROSTHETIC	BOASTING	INTENSITY	RUMMY	AMPUTATED
CONTINGENCY	CONJUGATIONS	BANKRUPTCY	PEROSHKIS	DECREPIT

Izzy, Willy-Nilly Vocabulary

NEEDLEPOINT	SOLITAIRE	KOWTOW	EDIBLE	GROUSED
SHALLOW	INCONVENIENT	GALE	REASSURANCE	DECREPIT
TRAUMA	EMPHATICALLY	FREE SPACE	FIBULA	PEROSHKIS
BLAND	SUBTLETY	CONDEMNED	TOUCHE	ANTAGONIZE
DIVERSIONARY	BOISTEROUS	ANGORA	BOASTING	PRECONCEPTIONS

Izzy, Willy-Nilly Vocabulary

IRRELEVANT	INADVERTENTLY	BATIK	GLYCERIN	ILLUSION
PRIVILEGED	AMPUTATED	REPRESSING	NAUTILUS	BANKRUPTCY
OBJECTIONS	JUVENILE	FREE SPACE	GENOISE	REPERTOIRE
OBJECTIVE	PREJUDICES	MARINATING	NECROSIS	NEGOTIATE
STABILIZED	THERAPY	SARCASM	RUMMY	LIBERATED

Izzy, Willy-Nilly Vocabulary

STABILIZED	INCOMPETENT	SHEEN	RUMMY	CERTIFIABLE
KOWTOW	IRRELEVANT	EMPHATICALLY	PREJUDICES	LIVERY
OBJECTIVE	DISJOINTED	FREE SPACE	INDEFINITE	PEAKED
INDENTURED	TRAUMA	AMPUTATED	WOES	REPERTOIRE
DIVERSIONARY	NOTORIOUS	INADVERTENTLY	ILLUSION	LINZERTORTE

Izzy, Willy-Nilly Vocabulary

DEFLATED	DWINDLED	WAILING	PSYCHOLOGICAL	PRECONCEPTIONS
IDEALIZE	SOLITARY	JUVENILE	INTRUDING	SHALLOW
RELUCTANCE	REPRESSING	FREE SPACE	ANTAGONIZE	AVULSED
GROUSED	BANKRUPTCY	CATHETER	EDIBLE	BOISTEROUS
GENOISE	SMOLDERING	BATIK	SOLITAIRE	NECROSIS

Izzy, Willy-Nilly Vocabulary

GLYCERIN	OBLIGE	ANEMIA	INCOMPETENT	CONTINGENCY
BLAND	CONTUSIONS	THERAPY	MARINATING	INADVERTENTLY
ILLUSION	NOTORIOUS	FREE SPACE	ANTAGONIZE	BANKRUPTCY
PRIVILEGED	GALE	INDEFINITE	EDIBLE	PSYCHOLOGICAL
DISJOINTED	CONJUGATIONS	LIBERATED	PROSTHETIC	SMOLDERING

Izzy, Willy-Nilly Vocabulary

KOWTOW	SOLITAIRE	CONVENIENT	DOMESTIC	BOASTING
PEDIATRICIAN	AMPUTATED	SOLITARY	FIBULA	WOES
PEAKED	CERTIFIABLE	FREE SPACE	DWINDLED	EVICT
OBJECTIVE	STABILIZED	EMPHATICALLY	IDEALIZE	INCONVENIENT
GENOISE	ANGORA	SHALLOW	TOUCHE	REPRESSING

Izzy, Willy-Nilly Vocabulary

OBLIGE	VANITY	PEROSHKIS	INDENTURED	BOASTING
PSYCHOLOGICAL	PROSTHETIC	TOUCHE	NOTORIOUS	BANKRUPTCY
INTRUDING	DECREPIT	FREE SPACE	UNDERESTIMATES	EDIBLE
IDEALIZE	NECROSIS	SUBTLETY	MARINATING	LIVERY
INCOMPETENT	WAILING	CONDEMNED	ANTAGONIZE	GENOISE

Izzy, Willy-Nilly Vocabulary

LIBERATED	KOWTOW	CERTIFIABLE	NAUTILUS	DIMINUTIVE
SOLITAIRE	CONJUGATIONS	IRRELEVANT	BLAND	PREJUDICES
WOES	CATHETER	FREE SPACE	CONTUSIONS	CONVENIENT
AMPUTATED	OBJECTIONS	GLYCERIN	GROUSED	PRECONCEPTIONS
THERAPY	SHEEN	FIBULA	DEFLATED	DISJOINTED

Izzy, Willy-Nilly Vocabulary

TOUCHE	SOLITARY	OBJECTIVE	REPRESSING	DIVERSIONARY
INADVERTENTLY	LINZERTORTE	CONVENIENT	BOISTEROUS	PRIVILEGED
SARCASM	ANEMIA	FREE SPACE	WAILING	NEGOTIATE
STABILIZED	HUMILIATION	DOMESTIC	CONTUSIONS	LIBERATED
KOWTOW	ANGORA	RELUCTANCE	SUBTLETY	LIVERY

Izzy, Willy-Nilly Vocabulary

EDIBLE	VANITY	PEDIATRICIAN	CONTINGENCY	GALE
NAUTILUS	NECROSIS	FIBULA	CERTIFIABLE	SOLITAIRE
MARINATING	SHALLOW	FREE SPACE	PSYCHOLOGICAL	INCOMPETENT
CONJUGATIONS	SHEEN	NEEDLEPOINT	THERAPY	DIMINUTIVE
GROUSED	AVULSED	TRAUMA	NOTORIOUS	PRECONCEPTIONS

Izzy, Willy-Nilly Vocabulary

GENOISE	DISJOINTED	FIBULA	GROUSED	UNDERESTIMATES
LIBERATED	PEAKED	HUMILIATION	ANEMIA	DWINDLED
JUVENILE	SHEEN	FREE SPACE	SOLITAIRE	PRECONCEPTIONS
VANITY	RELUCTANCE	BOASTING	IRRELEVANT	INDEFINITE
GALE	AVULSED	PEROSHKIS	DIVERT	BLAND

Izzy, Willy-Nilly Vocabulary

PEDIATRICIAN	ILLUSION	DECREPIT	STABILIZED	PSYCHOLOGICAL
CONTINGENCY	CONTUSIONS	CATHETER	INTRUDING	IDEALIZE
INDENTURED	LIVERY	FREE SPACE	WAILING	SOLITARY
SUBTLETY	INCONVENIENT	AMPUTATED	EVICT	CONJUGATIONS
PREJUDICES	BATIK	EDIBLE	INCOMPETENT	WOES

Izzy, Willy-Nilly Vocabulary

REPRESSING	SOLITARY	LIBERATED	PROSTHETIC	ANEMIA
STABILIZED	GALE	BANKRUPTCY	DWINDLED	CONDEMNED
SHALLOW	ANTAGONIZE	FREE SPACE	HUMILIATION	NECROSIS
INDENTURED	SHEEN	DIVERT	GROUSED	DOMESTIC
WOES	GENOISE	PSYCHOLOGICAL	JUVENILE	BATIK

Izzy, Willy-Nilly Vocabulary

PEROSHKIS	CERTIFIABLE	BOISTEROUS	SOLITAIRE	PRIVILEGED
FIBULA	INCOMPETENT	LIVERY	PEDIATRICIAN	OBLIGE
ANGORA	DEFLATED	FREE SPACE	KOWTOW	EVICT
NOTORIOUS	MARINATING	DISJOINTED	VANITY	AMPUTATED
SUBTLETY	REPERTOIRE	REASSURANCE	BOASTING	TOUCHE

Izzy, Willy-Nilly Vocabulary

LINZERTORTE	GALE	WAILING	DIMINUTIVE	DIVERT
SMOLDERING	DEFLATED	PREJUDICES	CONDEMNED	CATHETER
BATIK	PROSTHETIC	FREE SPACE	ANGORA	DISJOINTED
OBJECTIONS	BANKRUPTCY	CERTIFIABLE	FIBULA	STABILIZED
PRIVILEGED	NEEDLEPOINT	BOISTEROUS	SHALLOW	GENOISE

Izzy, Willy-Nilly Vocabulary

REPRESSING	INDENTURED	BLAND	HUMILIATION	REASSURANCE
NEGOTIATE	DOMESTIC	TRAUMA	DWINDLED	EMPHATICALLY
INTRUDING	LIVERY	FREE SPACE	INCONVENIENT	EVICT
INCOMPETENT	OBJECTIVE	EDIBLE	CONVENIENT	NOTORIOUS
KOWTOW	INTENSITY	PRECONCEPTIONS	TOUCHE	RELUCTANCE

Izzy, Willy-Nilly Vocabulary

BOISTEROUS	AVULSED	NECROSIS	RUMMY	STABILIZED
WOES	CONJUGATIONS	THERAPY	PSYCHOLOGICAL	DECREPIT
SARCASM	BLAND	FREE SPACE	LIBERATED	GROUSED
NAUTILUS	DIMINUTIVE	MARINATING	LIVERY	NEEDLEPOINT
TRAUMA	DOMESTIC	GENOISE	PEAKED	INTENSITY

Izzy, Willy-Nilly Vocabulary

DIVERT	INDEFINITE	EMPHATICALLY	CERTIFIABLE	REPERTOIRE
INDENTURED	OBLIGE	INTRUDING	GALE	REPRESSING
EDIBLE	EVICT	FREE SPACE	INCONVENIENT	INADVERTENTLY
PRIVILEGED	NEGOTIATE	SUBTLETY	PRECONCEPTIONS	DWINDLED
SHEEN	HUMILIATION	BOASTING	SOLITARY	VANITY

Izzy, Willy-Nilly Vocabulary

STABILIZED	TRAUMA	PEROSHKIS	NAUTILUS	PEDIATRICIAN
DIMINUTIVE	BOASTING	GALE	DWINDLED	REASSURANCE
ANTAGONIZE	SMOLDERING	FREE SPACE	RELUCTANCE	HUMILIATION
CONTINGENCY	FIBULA	UNDERESTIMATES	SUBTLETY	INTENSITY
SHALLOW	RUMMY	DOMESTIC	PREJUDICES	REPRESSING

Izzy, Willy-Nilly Vocabulary

SARCASM	DIVERT	BOISTEROUS	BANKRUPTCY	SOLITARY
IDEALIZE	CONDEMNED	PRECONCEPTIONS	INCOMPETENT	CONTUSIONS
ANEMIA	LIVERY	FREE SPACE	OBJECTIVE	DECREPIT
PROSTHETIC	CONVENIENT	INADVERTENTLY	ANGORA	INDENTURED
SHEEN	TOUCHE	KOWTOW	DEFLATED	GENOISE

Izzy, Willy-Nilly Vocabulary

SOLITARY	RUMMY	UNDERESTIMATES	VANITY	EMPHATICALLY
NEEDLEPOINT	ANTAGONIZE	CONDEMNED	SHALLOW	NECROSIS
STABILIZED	REPERTOIRE	FREE SPACE	INADVERTENTLY	TRAUMA
CERTIFIABLE	RELUCTANCE	INCOMPETENT	PREJUDICES	AVULSED
JUVENILE	FIBULA	GROUSED	INDENTURED	WAILING

Izzy, Willy-Nilly Vocabulary

SMOLDERING	PRECONCEPTIONS	PEAKED	LIBERATED	HUMILIATION
REASSURANCE	DOMESTIC	DIMINUTIVE	BATIK	OBLIGE
CATHETER	DECREPIT	FREE SPACE	OBJECTIONS	CONTUSIONS
AMPUTATED	IDEALIZE	PEDIATRICIAN	LIVERY	DIVERT
BOASTING	IRRELEVANT	THERAPY	INCONVENIENT	GLYCERIN

Izzy, Willy-Nilly Vocabulary

VANITY	IRRELEVANT	WAILING	INTRUDING	PRECONCEPTIONS
CERTIFIABLE	AVULSED	IDEALIZE	BOISTEROUS	ANGORA
DISJOINTED	CONJUGATIONS	FREE SPACE	PEDIATRICIAN	PEROSHKIS
EVICT	CONDEMNED	DEFLATED	BATIK	PSYCHOLOGICAL
SOLITAIRE	FIBULA	DOMESTIC	NOTORIOUS	THERAPY

Izzy, Willy-Nilly Vocabulary

SOLITARY	DWINDLED	REPRESSING	NECROSIS	INDEFINITE
HUMILIATION	ILLUSION	DIVERT	REPERTOIRE	WOES
CONVENIENT	ANEMIA	FREE SPACE	MARINATING	INADVERTENTLY
ANTAGONIZE	NAUTILUS	SHEEN	INTENSITY	BANKRUPTCY
PEAKED	GLYCERIN	NEEDLEPOINT	CATHETER	DIMINUTIVE

Izzy, Willy-Nilly Vocabulary

CERTIFIABLE	DIVERT	SMOLDERING	PRECONCEPTIONS	TRAUMA
SUBTLETY	INCONVENIENT	SOLITAIRE	PEROSHKIS	IDEALIZE
BOISTEROUS	PROSTHETIC	FREE SPACE	REPERTOIRE	ANTAGONIZE
CONVENIENT	INCOMPETENT	TOUCHE	EVICT	DOMESTIC
DWINDLED	NOTORIOUS	DISJOINTED	PREJUDICES	CONTINGENCY

Izzy, Willy-Nilly Vocabulary

WOES	FIBULA	INTRUDING	BOASTING	EDIBLE
NEGOTIATE	LIVERY	LIBERATED	BANKRUPTCY	ILLUSION
OBJECTIVE	RUMMY	FREE SPACE	INADVERTENTLY	IRRELEVANT
CATHETER	JUVENILE	BATIK	WAILING	PSYCHOLOGICAL
GALE	EMPHATICALLY	DECREPIT	RELUCTANCE	UNDERESTIMATES